A HISTORY OF

BENTLEY WOOD

The Friends of Bentley Wood

A Survey of BENTLEY WOODs in the Parish of West-Dean in the County of WILTS Belonging to His Grace the Duke of Queensberry and Dover.

H. Fllteroft fecit
1726

The cartouche from the 1726 map of Bentley Wood. Photo - A Baskerville.

A HISTORY OF

BENTLEY WOOD

Margaret Baskerville and David Lambert

With Peter Scrivens

Drawings by Roger Pearce

The Friends of Bentley Wood

With gratitude to the many people who have
contributed to the following pages

First published in 2005 by The Friends of Bentley Wood

Bentley Wood Trust C/o Hale Farm, Hale, Fordingbridge. SP6 2RD

ISBN 0-9550853-0-6

©Baskerville, Lambert & Scrivens

Baskerville, Lambert & Scrivens have asserted their rights under the Copyright,
Designs and Patent Act 1988 to be identified as the authors of this work

Printed and bound by The Baskerville Press Ltd., Salisbury, Wiltshire

A CIP catalogue record for this book is available from the British library

Local Heritage *initiative*

Contents

Acknowledgements

The Local History Group is part of The Friends of Bentley Wood and this book has been produced on their behalf. Many people have helped us to bring together the material for the book, by giving their time and permission to reproduce illustrations, and we would particularly like to thank the following:

Arthur Baskerville for many of the photographs and his help in reading the manuscript, Ordnance Survey, The Dean and Chapter of Salisbury Cathedral, B. and J. Davies (timber merchants, Shropshire), Salisbury Newspaper Group and N. Sampford for permission to reproduce illustrations, Chris Walker for permission to reproduce extracts from John Parsons' book and Graham Bathe for unearthing material from the Longleat archives.

We are particularly indebted to both Wiltshire and Hampshire Record offices, Salisbury Library Local Studies Section and the Chris Trower New Forest Reference Library, Lyndhurst, for permission to print the illustrations as indicated, and for the unfailing help, encouragement and patience of their staff.

Local historians Michael Parsons, David Parrott and Norman Thorne have given their advice and guidance on many occasions, for which we are very grateful.

We would like to thank the former staff of Norman Court estate and the Forestry Commission as well as the residents of the local villages, who gave their reminiscences and photographs so freely and enthusiastically.

We would particularly like to thank the Trustees of Bentley Wood for their help and encouragement.

Although many people have helped us to gather the material together, it has only been possible to produce it in its present form thanks to a Local Heritage Initiative grant, administered by the Countryside Agency.

Introduction

Bentley Wood lies in the south-east corner of Wiltshire, almost on the Hampshire border, and a few miles distant from Salisbury (Fig.1).The area of woodland, 1700 acres in extent, was purchased by the late Lady Colman of Winterslow in 1983 and is now managed by a Charitable Trust. The Trust have developed the wood as a nature reserve and amenity area, in addition to managing it for timber production. There is a rich and varied ground flora in the more open areas, and the wood has been designated a Site of Special Scientific Interest (SSSI) because of the range of Lepidoptera which it supports.

The wood straddles the sharp division between the chalk downland to the north and the Hampshire basin to the south, so that the underlying geology varies considerably in different parts of the wood. The northern part is mainly well-drained chalk, whereas much of the south is heavy clay, with a band of chalk again on the southern extremity. This gives a wide variation in soil type, which has a major effect on the vegetation which grows there, and the general character of the wood. Soil structure also affects the ease, or otherwise, of working the land. Throughout history this was a factor in determining which parts were cultivated, and which remained as woodland.

The public have free access to walk throughout the wood, and many people, both from the local villages and from further afield, regularly enjoy a walk there. Some come to exercise their dogs and children, others to study the flora and fauna and the rest just to enjoy the peaceful scenery.

It is for the many people who enjoy being in the wood, for whatever reason, that we have produced this book. It can only add to the pleasure of a walk to know a little about the people who have been there before, and to wonder how the wood might have looked to the Romano-British farmer, the medieval huntsman, or the 19th century woodland labourer. It is also important to collect together the information, pictures, records and memories of the wood from the 20th century, before it is too late and they are lost for ever. The history of Bentley Wood is a long and interesting one; we hope that you will enjoy it.

1

In The Beginning

The history of our wood has no real starting point. The geology and climate of Britain have changed dramatically over millions of years as part of global developments on a vast time scale, changes which are still going on today. It seems most appropriate to start at the end of the last Ice Age, about 11,000 BC, a short time ago in geological terms, but a very long time when compared with history since the Roman conquest.

As the climate improved after the Ice Age, the tundra waste lands of southern Britain were invaded by trees and a dense blanket of forest developed. The tree species which predominated in this 'wildwood' are known from analysis of pollen which has been preserved in places where the conditions were suitable, such as peat bogs. Over about 5,500 years, as it became warmer, the early colonizers, birch, aspen and sallow, gave way to pine and hazel. Alder and oak followed, and then lime and elm; to these were added beech and ash, holly, maple and hornbeam. Pine subsequently died out completely, and remained absent until it was introduced in the 18th century. Pollen samples also show that elm declined dramatically in the Neolithic period, to recover again in historical times. The decline coincided with the clearance of woodland by man for agriculture, but it was so rapid and so widespread that disease may have been an important contributing factor[1].

Fallen trees would have produced small clearings in the dense, dark forest, which allowed light to penetrate once again to the forest floor, and more trees gradually grew up to fill the gap. From time to time there would have been larger clearings; devastation similar to that caused by the great storms of 1987 and 1990 may not have been uncommon. Smaller plants had the opportunity to flourish in these natural clearings for a while, providing food for deer and wild cattle, until the trees grew and the light was reduced again.

As the land gradually warmed up after the Ice Age and the forests expanded, the animals which had been driven south by the icy conditions moved northwards again into new feeding grounds. Behind them came man, in search of the red and roe deer, pigs, aurochs and elk to supplement his diet of vegetable food and nuts. To start with, man and animals could move in freely, but by about 7,000BC the sea levels had changed, the lowland plains to the south of us became the English Channel, and Britain became an island. Early man would have had very little effect on the forests that covered southern Britain, but these hunter-gatherers did have fire as a way of manipulating their environment, in addition to their stone and flint tools. Clearings caused by fire provided grazing for the animals they were hunting, which if the animals were sufficiently numerous, delayed the return of the tree cover. Some trees regenerate more quickly than others, and hazel, for example, would have been favoured by forest fires. The nuts were a valuable food source and hazel is thought to have been encouraged in this primitive way[2].

The weapons and tools used before the discovery and development of metals were made from natural, easily available hard substances, flint and stone, antler and bone. Flint was an obvious choice in areas where it was plentiful, and patches of clay-with-flints were favoured places for collecting them; skilful working then produced very effective instruments. Surface flints are prone to frost damage and the best specimens are to be found deep within the undisturbed chalk where they occur in layers. In Neolithic times flint mines were dug using antler picks in order to extract them. The flint mines on Easton Down are just a few miles to the north of Bentley Wood. Flint is almost indestructible when lying in any type of soil, and some of the weapons which were fashioned so long ago can still be found throughout Wessex today.

About 4000BC man began to have a more dramatic effect on the forests; he became a farmer rather than a hunter. He discovered how to cultivate the ground to grow food crops, and how to domesticate some animal species. There was no longer any need to be constantly on the move searching for naturally-produced food, and stalking free-moving herds of wild animals. Permanent dwellings naturally followed, and social organisation became necessary for the smooth-running of the farming enterprise. These early farmers began the systematic clearance of the forest which in a few thousand years dramatically changed the landscape for ever. They cleared areas for growing crops and for grazing their animals. Continued use of a clearing without replacing the nutrients with manure soon depleted the soil, and another area had to be cleared to replace it. The chalk uplands were the easiest ground to break up and cultivate with the primitive tools available at that time and large areas of Wiltshire became open downland. Lower-lying, wetter ground and heavy clay soils remained as forest. Over the long time scale which we are considering the

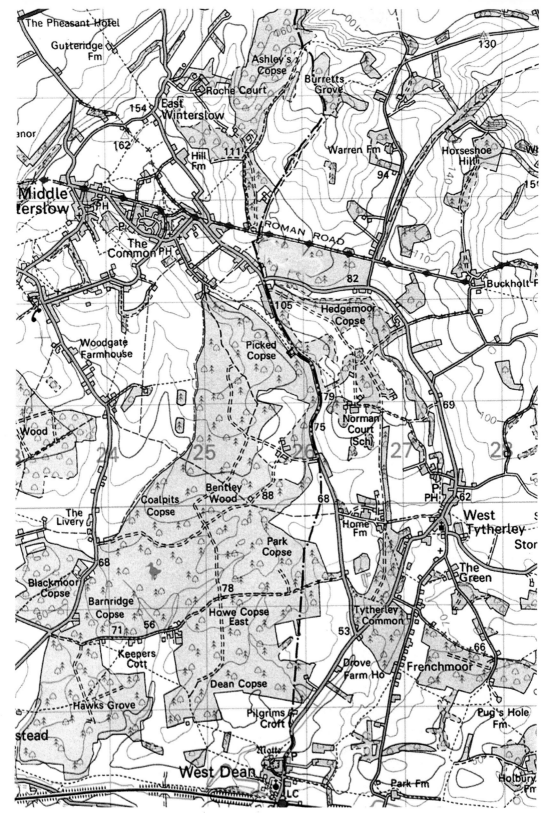

Fig 1 *Bentley Wood and the surrounding villages (OS Landranger map 184, 1984).*
Crown copyright. All rights reserved. Licence no. WL8103.

4

forest would have waxed and waned in extent, but the pattern of large open areas interspersed with woodland had been set.

Most of the traces of prehistoric peoples that still exist today are found on the chalk upland. It was there that they built their ceremonial gathering places and monuments to their dead. Many of these lay only a day's journey to the north of Bentley Wood, and any families living in this area must have looked northwards towards Salisbury Plain as the cultural centre of their society.

During the last century BC defensive structures appeared on some of the hilltops in the area; tribal warfare was an endemic state which lasted until peace was enforced by the Romans. The hillfort at Figsbury Rings and the camp at Ashley's Copse are both within two or three miles of Bentley Wood and it is possible that during the Iron Age some of the lighter land around the wood was being utilized for pastoral purposes. Sheep were kept in increasing numbers as they could graze on the open downland far from a source of water.

In spite of the extensive clearance, woodland remained important to prehistoric communities. Their cattle and pigs fed there, they still harvested the nuts from the hazel, and they also needed the hazel and alder to build their

Fig 2 *A wild boar. (R Pearce)*

circular wattle houses. By the end of the Iron Age the management of hazel and alder by coppicing was widespread[3]. Wild animals still roamed there, and some would have been hunted; they would have provided a useful addition to the diet, especially in winter.

The wildlife which existed in the woodland gradually changed over the centuries. The elk and the bear became extinct at an early stage, but some other species, such as the beaver, lingered on in a few places into historic times. Wolves and wild boar would have been present in Bentley Wood and did not disappear until the Middle Ages. The wild swine looked very similar to the early domestic pigs and interbred with them. Both the formidable aurochs and the smaller wild cattle *(Bos longifrons)* were the ancestors of later domestic cattle, and the original wild forms became extinct.

We have no direct knowledge of what Bentley Wood was like on the eve of the Roman conquest. However, it is thought that the climate was very cold and wet during the Iron Age, so that the southern part of the wood and the Dean valley, which was probably still woodland, were likely to have been waterlogged and difficult to penetrate for a prolonged period. It is possible that the northern part of the wood, on the lighter chalk soil, may have been partially cleared at that time and utilized by local farm settlements.

2

Roman Times

The Roman conquest and settlement of Britain brought about many changes to the landscape. Instead of small settlements of thatched wooden huts, large houses and stone buildings were constructed, long straight roads crossed the countryside and towns and cities were developed. The native population still had their small settlements, but some of them prospered under Roman rule and were able to adopt the new way of life which the Romans had introduced.

During the period of Roman occupation, AD43-410, Romano-British villas owned by native Britons became widespread in southern England. The Latin word villa means "a rural dwelling with associated farm buildings". It was not just a country house, but the centre of an agricultural estate which usually consisted of a mixed arable and livestock farming enterprise.

The presence of the Roman army in Britain, and the development of towns which were not agriculturally self-sufficient, greatly increased the requirement for grain production. This deficit had to be met by farms producing a surplus over and above their own requirements, and would have provided a market stimulus for them to do so[1]. The good new road network made it possible for farm produce to be transported to markets some distance away.

The Romans utilized the improvements in farming methods which had been emerging among Iron Age cultures at that time. Earlier settlers had had to confine their agricultural activities to the light chalk soils on the downland, whereas the Romans were able to break up heavier ground. Their iron industry helped in this, and they built more robust and efficient ploughs. The two-handed scythe and the sickle were introduced so that cereal and hay crops could be harvested more easily. Cereals grown in Britain at that time included spelt and bread wheats, barley, oats and rye; pulses, flax and hemp were also grown[2]. In addition to arable crops, Romano-British farms included the usual range of domestic animals, particularly sheep, cattle, pigs, horses and poultry. Cattle, rather than horses, were the animal species used for ploughing and transport. Roman farming techniques were sufficiently advanced to carry out land drainage, to rotate crops and to use manure to increase the fertility of the soil[2].

Fig 3 *East Grimstead Roman villa as it might have looked in the 4th century AD. (R Pearce)*

The Dean valley to the south of Bentley Wood provided an ideal site for Roman farming activities. The valley gravel soil was particularly fertile and there was easy access to both chalk and clay land. The river Dun provided a water source and there were readily available supplies of wood all along the north side of the valley. The new road from Sorviodunum (Old Sarum) to Venta Belgarum (Winchester) was within easy reach. Such ideal conditions allowed three villa estates, East Grimstead, West Dean and Holbury to operate in unusually close proximity to each other[3]. The East Grimstead villa lies immediately adjacent to the southern boundary of Bentley Wood (Fig.33). These Romano-British villas would have been thriving concerns surrounded by extensive arable, grazing and meadow areas.

Early Roman villas were timber, or half-timbered and brick buildings and the Grimstead and West Dean villas may initially have been constructed in this way. Stone was used in the later part of the Roman period. The excavated remains of the West Dean villa walls were of flint construction with some stone, and Portland stone roof tiles were also found on the site[4]. Wood and clay would have been available locally. The buildings were a considerable size; Grimstead, which was excavated in 1924 by Heywood Sumner, was an aisled house 50 by 140 feet in extent and included a hypocaust heating system[5] (Fig.3). There were also three bath suites, a degree of luxury not seen again in East Grimstead for nearly 2000 years (Fig.4)! At West Dean three separate buildings were found, also with hypocaust heating and baths. A mosaic floor had been found in 1741, a hundred years before the main excavations[4].

Such extensive and elaborate buildings and farming enterprises would have had a considerable impact on the countryside around, particularly as there were three villas close together. The Dean valley was cleared for agricultural land, and the remaining woodland, including Bentley Wood, would have been the source of wood. Central heating and three bathrooms came at a price; it created an endless requirement for fuel. Large timber was needed for building construction and repair, and smaller wood for fences and hurdles for animal enclosures. Many tools, farm implements and household equipment were also made of wood. The fuel needed would have been considerable; apart from cooking and heating, bricks and tiles were probably made from local clay and fired on site, and the blacksmith would have needed heat for metal working.

In Prehistoric times man had recognised that when deciduous trees were cut down the root did not die. A number of shoots soon appeared on the stump

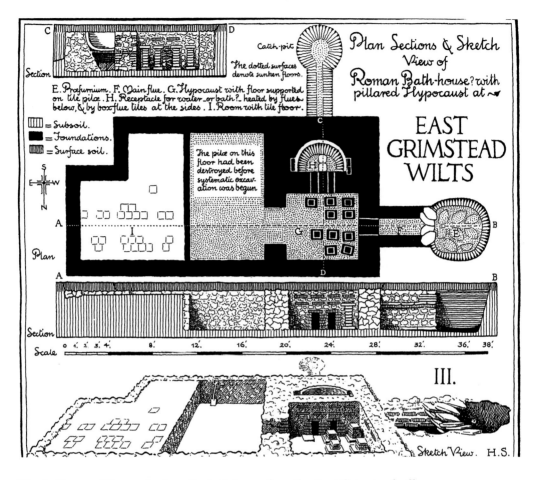

Fig 4 *Heywood Sumner's plan of a bath house from the East Grimstead villa.*

which, within a few years, produced several small trees from the coppiced "stool". This was a useful way of producing long straight poles for making hurdles, which had been exploited during the Iron Age. Repeatedly coppicing the stools of trees to produce a crop of wood every few years was not particularly important when early communities had abundant untouched woodland in the immediate locality. They also wanted to pull out the tree roots and increase the area of land available for agriculture. Eventually, large parts of southern England were denuded of woodland, particularly the chalk downlands. The regular coppicing of hazel, ash, lime, alder and other tree species at intervals of 5-10 years, gradually came to be recognised as the most efficient means of producing a dependable supply of wood for most purposes. A few trees, particularly oaks, could be reserved for the production of larger timber and allowed to grow into "standards".

It is not known in detail how the Romans managed their woodland in Britain[6], but they are thought to have used it as a renewable resource as the only way of providing for their requirements. In addition to normal domestic use, their iron, pottery and glass industries consumed prodigious quantities of wood and charcoal. They are known to have coppiced wood in their native homeland, and their use of wattle for building in Britain implies the production of suitable rods from hazel coppice stools[2]. The Romans introduced chestnut trees into Britain but there is no local evidence of this. They also brought in many plants which we still have in our gardens today. The forestry tools available at that time included iron axes, saws and billhooks; not so very different from those in current use. Ox carts were used for transporting the wood.

We can only hazard a guess at what the woodland region, later to become Bentley Wood, would have looked like in those early times. Clearly, for about 400 years the three villas used considerable quantities of wood and they probably obtained it locally. Much previously undisturbed woodland must have been felled in the surrounding area. Initially, in such a heavily wooded region, there may not have been a great need for coppice management, but it is possible that it was carried out during the later part of the period. Where the soil was suitable for agriculture in the Dean Valley itself, the trees were cleared, leaving woodland or scrub on the heavier ground, or on the steeper parts of Dean Hill. Much of the wood for the East Grimstead and West Dean villas was probably taken from the southern part of Bentley Wood, but they may have ranged further afield when looking for larger timber or a particular species of tree.

In addition to keeping domestic livestock, the owners of Roman villas often hunted wild animals, both for sport and for food and hunting scenes were often depicted on their pottery and mosaics. Deer, wild boar and wolves were all likely to have been present in and around Bentley Wood and they may well have been hunted by the inhabitants of the Dean valley villas. Red deer bones or antlers were found at all three villa sites[4,5,9] and G.S.Master[4] also found roe and fallow antlers at West Dean. However, this is not sufficient reliable evidence to say that fallow deer were roaming around Bentley Wood in Roman times.

The extent of woodland at the end of the Roman period can be estimated by the position of settlements with –ley, –field and –stead names, as they were Old English words meaning an area in the woodland cleared by the Saxons. In what was later to become Clarendon Forest, the area around Farley and the Grimsteads was therefore likely to have been continuous woodland in Roman times[7].

The climate during the centuries of Roman occupation would have had a major influence on what the countryside was like at that time. Even today slight differences have a considerable effect; just a few weeks of wet weather in winter leaves the southern part of Bentley Wood in a boggy state, with gushing streams, water lying in the surrounding fields and the Dun becomes a sizeable river. The evidence is rather conflicting, but the general trend seems to have been for the cold weather of the Iron Age to have improved throughout the Roman Period. Temperatures during the third and fourth centuries AD may have been slightly higher than the average today, with relatively dry summers[8].

3

The Early Owners Of The Wood

The Amesbury Connection

For much of its history Bentley Wood has been a separate part of the estate of the manor of Amesbury, which is ten miles away. In previous times the journey to Winterslow from Amesbury would have been long and arduous, so why should an estate retain an isolated piece of woodland?

Since the time when man first settled in southern England the commodities which were needed most vitally were water, food and wood. The woodland was gradually cleared from the higher ground as early settlers expanded the areas for food crops and pasture for animals; in doing so they provided themselves with wood for fuel and for building their dwellings, shelters and fences. In time this clearance left the chalk uplands, which were the easiest areas to clear and cultivate, with relatively little woodland. However, as human populations grew, there was a greater need than ever for wood. Woodland was also essential for harbouring wild animals which were a useful source of meat before man had learned how to provide adequate winter feed for his domestic animals. Until that time deer, and other wild animals, which could feed themselves in winter, were an invaluable source of food. The domestic animal used most commonly for meat was the pig, and pannage, or the turning out of pigs into woodland to forage for acorns and beech mast, made it possible to raise pigs for slaughter with minimal use of grain which was a scarce resource.

This need for woodland is reflected in the way in which the large local estates were formed in Saxon times. To be viable an estate had to have the three vital features; water, land suitable for agriculture and woodland. Trade would have supplied anything else, such as salt or iron, but the estate needed to be self-sufficient in the basic materials. These essential requirements are one reason for the fragmented nature of estates, which often held geographically separate areas of land, or certain rights in such areas, to provide commodities which were unavailable nearer home. This need for woodland explains the interest in Bentley Wood by an estate on the southern edge of Salisbury plain where most of the woods had been cleared in earlier times.

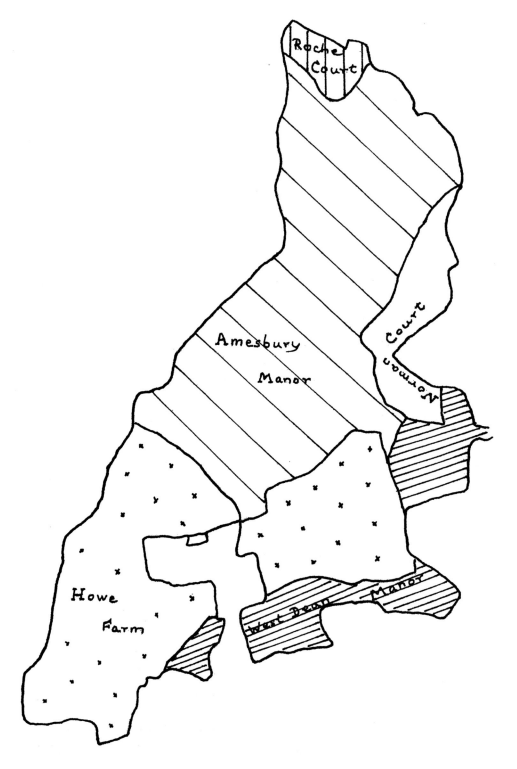

Fig 5 *The owners of Bentley Wood prior to the 19th century. (M Baskerville)*

The area around Amesbury had been an important centre of prehistoric civilisation and there are still the remains of a large Iron Age hill fort close to the present town. Amesbury continued to be an important regional centre following the settlement of the area by the Saxons. It is thought to have belonged to the rulers of Wessex as far back as the 7th century and was firmly established as a royal manor by the time of Alfred the Great. Amesbury manor continued to be held directly by the crown until the 1140s, being taken over by William the Conqueror from Edward the Confessor at the Norman Conquest. The Normans retained the administrative and tax collection systems which the Saxons had developed, whereby the country was divided up into shires and hundreds and Amesbury became the centre of the Amesbury hundred.

The Domesday Book credits the manor of Amesbury with 29,000 acres of woodland, a huge area which is thought to have included the whole of Clarendon Forest, as there was little or no woodland in the Amesbury area itself. In the 1140s Amesbury manor ceased to be held by the Crown and was passed to the Earl of Salisbury. From that time onwards it no longer included such large tracts of land separated from the manor. However, Bentley Wood, together with a stretch of woodland in East Winterslow (the Noad's Copse and Ramshill area), remained part of Amesbury manor until the 1820s, as the estate needed to retain a source of wood. The "ownership" of Bentley Wood therefore follows the history of the manor of Amesbury. Although no longer a royal estate, it was always held by one of the most powerful noblemen in the country. Initially the whole of Bentley Wood as we know it today belonged to Amesbury, but from 1227 the estate included the northern part of the wood only (Fig.5).

Estates in medieval times were the king's gift to his subjects in return for their support and military service. The most influential subjects, the barons, held many estates in different parts of the country. They would not necessarily have spent much time there; in many cases they would have used the estate as a source of revenue and only visited periodically, perhaps for a hunting expedition. Amesbury, however, was situated close to the Norman and Plantagenet kings' main palace at Winchester and to Clarendon, and was therefore probably fairly central to the lord's activities. Unfortunately, with great power came the increased likelihood of a rapid fall in one's fortunes. Some of the holders of Amesbury were beheaded, having fallen out of favour, or backed the wrong side in the struggle for the crown. Edward Seymour, Earl of Hertford and Duke of Somerset, ruled England as Lord Protector during the reign of Edward VI, who became king when only nine years old. In addition to his other estates, Seymour held the manor of Amesbury, and an account for Bentley Wood (App. IV) has been found among his papers. Despite his exalted position he had a series of disputes with other powerful noblemen surrounding the king, and having been tried by his peers, he was convicted of felony and executed in 1553. The Seymour 1540 rent roll for Bentley Wood provides the earliest account of what the wood looked like at that time as it lists commons, or open areas, separately from coppices. It also gives the coppices and grazing land in the Noad's Copse and Ramshill area among the Bentley Wood coppices, showing that it was all managed as one combined estate.

A more interesting fate befell the Duke of Clarence, who held Amesbury estate as his wife's inheritance; having been condemned to death in1478, he is thought to have ended his days drowned in a butt of malmsey (Madeira wine).

Although all land was "held" from the king rather than owned, titles and estates were inherited down the holder's family. However, when a holder died without issue, or forfeited the estate because he had opposed the king, it was taken back into royal custody and managed by stewards. The manor and title were then given as gifts to another baron. This was the pattern with Amesbury; at various times it returned to being a royal estate. On one occasion it was given to the Bishop of Winchester who used the estate to finance St Cross hospital. When a minor inherited the manor, the land was held and managed by a trustee until the heir was of age. Queen Eleanor held the estate during the childhood of Margaret Longespee from 1257 – 1268. Some 200 years later, when it was inherited by Edward Plantagenet, Earl of Warwick and son of the unfortunate Duke of Clarence, the manor was again in crown wardship and arrangements made to manage it. The following is recorded in 1485[2]:

Grant to John Hayes of the office of receiver of all lands in the counties of Cornwall, Devon, Somerset, Dorset, Wilts and Southampton called Salesburys lands and Spencers lands' with 20 marks a year from the issues thereof for his wages and fees: and of the keeping of the woods of Bentley and Melchette co Wilts, with the ancient and accustomed wages out of the lordship of Amesbury and Winterbourne: in the king's hands by the minority of Edward son of Isabel late the wife of George, late Duke of Clarence: to hold during the said minority.

Amesbury was also the site of an important Benedictine nunnery from 979AD. However, the abbey was not as wealthy as those of Wilton or Romsey and eventually also lost some of its land, such as a portion of Winterslow, to more powerful local estates. It had also lost royal favour at a time when the king, Henry II, was looking round for somewhere to found a new religious order. The Amesbury nuns seem to have indulged in a scandalous lifestyle. It was probably no worse than that of the rest of the population but such conduct in an Abbess and her followers could be prejudicial when the King was looking for an excuse to close them down. They were duly dismissed for their turpitude and depravity and Henry II was able to found his new order. This was to be a priory, a lower level than an abbey, and a troop of about 24 well-behaved nuns was imported from Fontevrault in France[3].

Henry granted the new nunnery wide-ranging rights in the area to provide a viable community. His first charter was probably issued in 1179, the contents of which are known from later charters which confirmed these rights[4]. The nuns were to hold the manors which their predecessors had held at Domesday and they were given, among other lands and tithes, the manor of Nether Wallop. They were also granted one cartload of wood per day from woodland in five different areas, Bentley, Wallop, Winterslow, Grovely and Chute.

Fig 6 *Hauling wood with oxen. (R Pearce)*

There is no indication as to whether one cartload of wood was fetched from Bentley on a daily basis throughout the year, or whether several carts appeared together at irregular intervals. It is known, however, that in 1271 six cartloads per week were being drawn from Bentley[2]. Prior's copse in Bentley Wood would seem to have been a likely area for taking at least some of the wood, and this suggests an entrance into the wood somewhere along the Tytherley Road of Winterslow. Such a steady demand for wood could easily have over-reached the sustainable production of the woodland, leaving large areas of "waste". Waste meant the denuding of woodland by excessive cutting and was a widespread medieval problem. It was an offence against Forest Law[5] but the nuns' charter specifically mentions that they could not be fined for waste.

A reference in the charter to the likely waste caused by a four-horsed vehicle suggests that horses could have been used for haulage and transport, but ox carts would seem more likely in the thirteenth century, especially if the wood was moved around during the winter months (Fig.6). Oxen were the main draught animal at that time and they pulled heavy loads across soft and heavy ground better than horses. An ox could work for several hours a day before needing a rest, and transported loads at a speed of 2-2$\frac{1}{2}$ miles an hour[6]. It did not require such a high energy diet as a horse, which was important when cereals for animal feed were scarce, and it could be used for meat when its working days were over. In later centuries bigger, stronger carthorses became available and these were better suited than oxen to hauling loads along firm road surfaces. Whichever the animal species used, such a regular use of the tracks on the nine or ten mile journey to Amesbury would have churned up the ground, particularly on the hills, and it may be that such transport was not possible during the worst part of the year.

In addition to the wood being taken to the Priory from Bentley, equivalent amounts were also being taken from Winterslow. In the thirteenth century Winterslow manor had 300 acres of woodland, mainly in Hound Wood, and in the area between Hound and Bentley woods[7]. A further daily cartload came from the nuns' Wallop estate, particularly from the Queen's Wood. A likely route to Amesbury for wood being transported from Prior's Copse and the eastern side of Bentley Wood would have been along Red Lane, Winterslow, and down the track to the present A30 road by the Pheasant Hotel. One has only to look at the steep holloway of Red Lane to realise that it has been made by frequent heavy use over many centuries. The most direct route would then have been along the old track across Idmiston Down to Idmiston. This would also have been used

Fig 7 *Domestic pigs enjoying pannage in Bentley Wood. (R Pearce)*

by traffic between Idmiston manor and the Shripple, Winterslow, where the manor held a detached portion of land. Wood from Hound Wood and the western part of Winterslow may have followed the Roman road and then gone over the downs to the Winterbournes. Either route involved a difficult journey, with steep hills for heavily- laden carts, and a crossing of the river Bourne.

The Amesbury nuns had another right in Bentley Wood which was established in their charter, the right of pannage for 100 pigs in the wood, for which they were exempt the pannage payment (Fig.7). Pannage, or the turning out of pigs to forage, provided an abundance of food for the pigs in the autumn when the acorns and beech mast had fallen, and it was traditionally allowed for about two months each year from the middle of September. In a heavily wooded area such as Hampshire large herds of swine were an important part of the rural economy[5]. Acorns are particularly nutritious, with a feeding value of about half that of barley. Although green acorns in large quantities cause toxicity problems in horses and cattle, pigs are not affected, and it is advantageous to have them

19

removed by this species. Beech mast is more fibrous, but is still a useful addition to the pig's diet. Free-ranging pigs also eat roots and rhizomes, particularly bracken and couch grass[8], and such a diet was invaluable for fattening up the pigs which were then slaughtered and the carcases salted before the winter. The pigs would have been overseen by a swineherd, who could have trained them to return to sleeping quarters or collecting yards. Nineteenth century swineherds were known to have done this[9], and in recent times in the New Forest, pigs on Bramshaw Common could be seen all wending their way back to the farmyard at the end of the day. The nuns'pigs may have joined with other pigs under the care of local swineherds. Pigs at that time would not have looked like the pigs which can be seen around the New Forest today; even the old traditional breeds, such as the Wessex Saddleback, were not developed until much later. Medieval pigs would have been rather like wild swine in appearance, long-legged, long-haired, razor-backed and probably dark-skinned[8]. Such pigs matured slowly, not reaching bacon weight until their third year.

Although the details are not known, it seems likely that cartloads of wood were also being taken on a regular basis from the northern part of Bentley Wood for use by the households of successive lords of the manor of Amesbury or their tenants. We do know, however, from reports of the forest eyres that the lord was sometimes fined for "waste" or felling the wood excessively (see Bentley in Clarendon Forest). The transportation methods and routes must have been the same as the wood going to the Priory. The manor probably also had its pigs in Bentley Wood during pannage time.

Wood continued to be an important commodity through the succeeding centuries. After the dissolution of the monasteries the priory was leased as a secular estate. In 1560 the lease included[10]:

All woods or fuel to be carried by two carts called " the bynne carts" with 3 horses in every cart going and coming every day in summer and winter in the woods and forests of Chute, Grovely and Benteley Woodde, for the wood to be brought to the site of the monastery, of old time accustomed.

In 1600 part of the Amesbury estate, which now included the Priory, was let by the holder, Sir Edward Seymour, Earl of Hertford, and the lease included[11].

To allow the lessee yearly for firebote (firewood) and hedgebote (fences) to be spent on the premises 1 acre of coppice wood standing, growing, renewing or being in or upon his coppices or coppice woods, parcel of Bentley Woodes co Wilts, when the earl shall fell or cut down the same, the felling, cutting down, making and carrying whereof shall be at the lessee's cost.

Another lease from the above earl in 1607 allowed "such necessary or old timber out of Bentley Woodes" to build a barn in Amesbury[12].

The Amesbury estate remained with the Seymour family until 1720 when it was sold to Lord Carleton. He left it to Charles Douglas, Duke of Queensberry in 1725 and a beautiful collection of maps of the estate, including Bentley Wood, was produced at this date (Fig.21)[13]. In the 1820s the estate was sold to Charles Baring Wall of Norman Court.

Howe Farm

Although agriculture and woodland were vital to the running of a rural estate, landowners in the 13th century had spiritual needs as well. Building churches, founding religious orders and endowing almshouses were regarded as important ways of ensuring the eternal salvation of a nobleman's soul. An early holder of Amesbury manor was William Longespee, illegitimate son of Henry II and half brother to the kings Richard I and John. Longespee wanted to build a large monastic establishment, and considered that the most suitable location would be the "Essart of Bentlewood". He created an assart, or cleared an area of woodland, towards the southern part of Bentley Wood in what was to become the later Howe Farm area, for his monastery. Unfortunately he died unexpectedly in 1225 but he left £200 in his will to build "St Mary of the Essart of Bentlewood". This was an even greater sum of money than that which he left towards the building of Salisbury Cathedral, which now houses his tomb (Fig.8); an indication of the importance which he attached to the intended project[14].

If it had not been for his untimely death the history of Bentley Wood would have been very different. His widow, Ela, Countess of Salisbury, must have decided against the idea, because in 1227 she endowed the Hospital of St Nicholas, an almshouse in Salisbury (Fig.9), with

all my enclosed land south of Bentlewood which remains after my gift to the persons of West Dean

(see The Southern Part of the Wood). This grant to the hospital included not only woods and clearings, meadows and pastures, roads and paths, but also 60

Fig 8 *The tomb of William Longespee in Salisbury Cathedral. (The Dean and Chapter). (photo. A Baskerville)*

cattle, 18 horses, 60 pigs and 30 sheep[15]. The animal numbers are interesting as they give an indication of what was needed for a self-contained estate to be viable. Ela then founded the abbey in Lacock instead of in Bentley Wood.

The original charter gave all the southern part of the wood to St. Nicholas' Hospital, except for the southern fringe which was given to West Dean manor. The boundary lines are shown in Fig. 5 and the map of Dean Wood of 1800[16]. The name Dean Wood was used during the 18th and 19th centuries when the term Bentley Wood was often used for the northern part of the wood only.

The Cartulary of St Nicholas' Hospital, a collection of their records, contains several references to their property, Howe Farm. The money and goods which the estate brought in helped to support 6 poor women and 6 poor men who were provided with food and shelter in the "hospital". The statutes of St Nicholas' Hospital include:

And also the said master shall find for the said brothers and sisters of the said house 16 waggon loads of wood yearly to be taken from the wood of The Howe and 1 waggon load of coals (charcoal) *each year.*

Charcoal produces little smoke and was used for heating large communal halls where there was no chimney.

In 1588 Howe Farm and woods were leased to Richard Zouch for 3 lives (the lease also extended to his wife and son), and the indenture for this lease[18] describes the area as coppice, coppicewood (coppice with standards), underwood and woody ground. Woody ground was likely to have been wood pasture, and underwood to have included pollards and all small trees, excluding oaks, which were not maintained as coppice. This early lease gives no precise indication as to where the coppice or woody ground lay, and just divides the land into North, South, East, West and Gilbert's coppices. Grazing rights for cattle throughout the coppices and woody ground were part of the lease. "Cattle" in this context could include other species of farm animals. All windfall trees could be taken by the tenant, whereas timber trees, and the underwood of "one good acre" of each coppice remained the property of St. Nicholas' Hospital. There were also rights of common, both the occupant of Howe farm and St. Nicholas' Hospital had had common grazing rights for cattle, and probably sheep, throughout the Amesbury Estate part of Bentley Wood, and also in Noad's Copse, Ramshill and Ashley copse "since time out of mind". The grazing period was from May 3rd until November 11th[24].

Fig 9 *St. Nicholas' Hospital, Salisbury (from Hall's Picturesque Memorials 1834)*

Later tenants who held Howe Farm include Sir John Evelyn, lord of the manor of West Dean, and the Duchess of Queensberry. The terms of these later leases were similar to the one described above, although some of the coppice

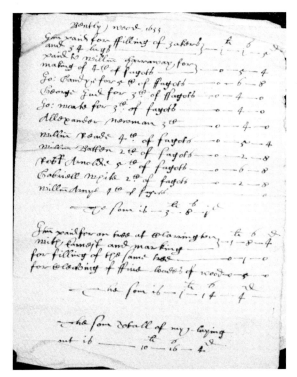

Fig 10 *A woodland account from the records of St Nicholas' Hospital (WCRO ref 1672/5/7) (photo A Baskerville)*

Bentley Wood 1633

	£	s	d
Item paid for filling of 3 akers and 34 lugs	1	1	5
Paid to William Harraway for making of 4C of fagots	0	5	4
Jo Gandy for 5C of fagots	0	6	8
George Jud for 3C of fagots	0	4	0
Jo Woate? for 3C of fagots	0	4	0
Alexander Neroman 3C	0	4	0
William Read 4C of fagots	0	5	4
William Batten 2C of fagots	0	2	8
Robert Arnold 5C of fagots	0	6	8
Gabriell White 2C of fagots	0	2	8
William Arnyl 1C of fagots			0

The Som is 3 8 1

	£	s	d
Item paid for or free at Clarington(Clarendon) with (?) and marking	1	8	4
for filling of the same	0	1	0
for cleaving of five loades of wood	0	4	0

The Som is 1 14 4

The som total of my laying
out is 10 16 4

names had changed. It is also apparent that by the late 18th century there was meadow land around the farm. The rights which went with the lease were given in more detail and included an allocation of wood for building purposes, for fencing and general repairs and for firewood. There was also permission to dig up roots and to carry away all the brambles, bushes and thorns. This was apparently a valuable perquisite in the 18th century!

A collection of correspondence in the St. Nicholas' Hospital records of 1614 show that relations between neighbouring owners in Bentley Wood were not always harmonious. The lord of Amesbury manor at that time was the all-powerful Edward Seymour, Earl of Hertford, who appears to have had some rather high-handed woodsmen in Bentley wood. The following petition from the Master of St. Nicholas' Hospital in 1614[19] to his Lordship accuses them of preventing access for cattle from Howe Farm to the grazing areas in Rowley, Blackmore Hill, Dean Heath, Ramshill and Bentley Wood. They had apparently also felled and sold the trees reserved for firewood for Howe Farm (Fig.11).

To the Right Honourable our very good Lord Edward Earl of Hertford.

In most humble wise complaining showeth unto your good Lordship your honourable daily (?) and poor suppliants The Master, chaplain and poor people of the hospital of Saint Nicholas in or near the city of New Sarum that whereas Ela, Countess of Sarum, by her deed dated 14 callens September 1227 did in pure alms give and grant unto the same hospital her assart or enclosure of Howe with one ground called Rowley and all the commons liberties and free customs and to the same belonging as in the same deed it doth more at large appear. And your said suppliants and their poor folk and their tenant by virtue of the same gift and grant have over time out of mind peaceably enjoyed both common of feeding and passage for their cattle in Howe Lane and in the said ground called Rowley, Bentley Wood, Dean Heath, Rams Hill and in all other commons, waste and coppices of your Lordship lying near the same wood. And also have ever lopped and shrowded the wood growing in the said lane and in Rowley for firewood for the tenement or house called Howe farm. Until of late years we and our tenants were first interrupted of our shrowdings and afterwards all the trees growing on the premises were felled and sold (except a very few small young ones) and also the herbage and pannage of one coppice called Rowley is enclosed and detained. And last of all both the same lane is laid so Barnridge coppice the hedge our bounds being taken away and the ground called Rowley is enclosed by your Lordships woodward and officers. Whereby we are deprived of our common there and passage to other common and of that wood have served the said farm and preserved the other store for the sustentation of the said hospital and poor people there who now in short time for lack of that which is taken away as is aforesaid are like to want. All which we presume and are verily persuaded hath been done without your Lordships knowledge and endured by us hitherto without complaint further than by entreaty to your Lordships said officer. Because the state of the said hospital was weak and especially because we had not until of late sight and knowledge of the original deed of the said Countess our honourable, charitable and merciful benefactress. Therefore now being well assured of your honourable, noble and godly inclination (much rather to help an almshouse than by any means to hurt or hinder it) we do most humbly crave that it may please your good honour to refer the hearing and examination of the cause to council or gentlemen of the country as your Lordship shall think fit. And upon their report out of your Lordships piety and love of the poor, to cause the poor hospital to be righted. And we and our successors shall be bound to pray to God for the comfort and prosperity of your honour and honourable house and posterity.

October 30 Anno 1614.

Your Honourable always to Command
Geffrey Bygge, Custos. Will'm Smegergyll, Capellanus.

Thomas Damary	*Mawd Roberts*
Walter Coleman	*Dorothey Cosard*
Nicholas Collins	*Joane Heath*
John Lyne	*Joane Bachelor*
Richard Weighte	*Agnes Vere*
Henry Alshawe	*Christian Nowell*

Poore aged people of St. Nicholas

Unfortunately the outcome of the dispute is not recorded, but it is noteworthy that by 1775 Rowley Marsh and Blackmore Hill (Fig. 12) had been allotted to Howe Farm "free on lease" instead of the common rights.

In 1677 a payment of £80 was received by the Hospital when a new lease was granted of Howe Farm and Woods. The money was spent on the maintenance of the hospital buildings and "defending it from repairing ye great bridge nere it", presumably construction work on the nearby Harnham bridge in Salisbury[17].

The ownership and usage of the area of Bentley called Dean Wood in the 17th and 18th centuries is not entirely clear. The acreages given for the

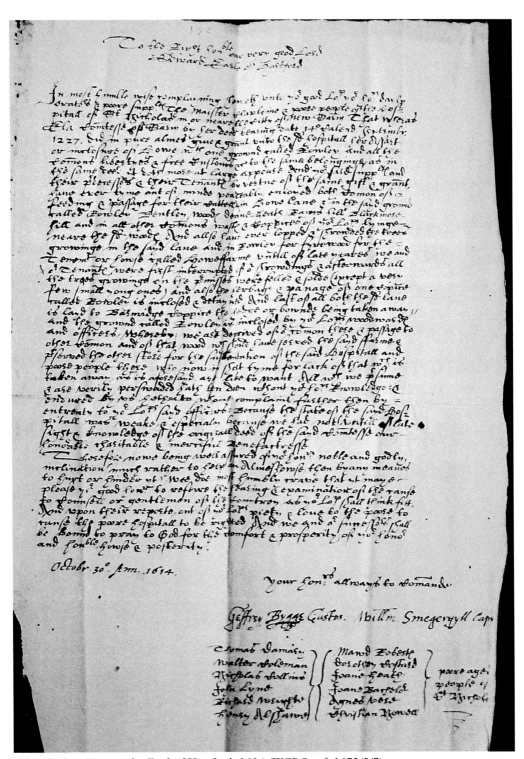

Fig 11 *A petition to the Earl of Hertford, 1614.(WCRO ref. 1672/5/7)*
(photo A Baskerville)

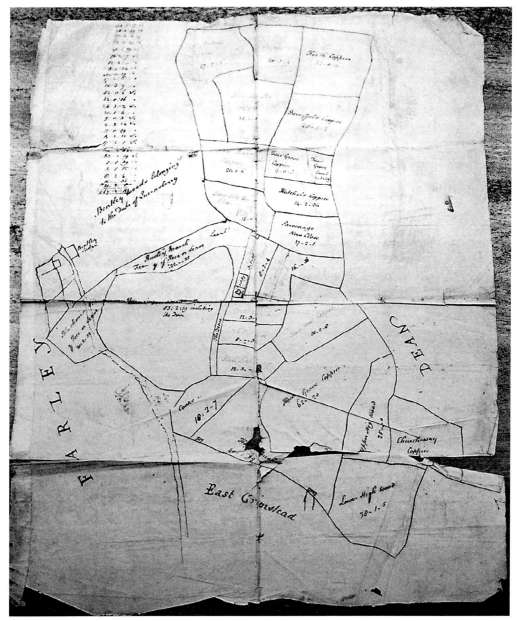

Fig 12 *Dean Wood circa 1800 (WCRO ref 727/13/10) (photo A Baskerville)*

woodland attached to Howe Farm in the early leases do not account for the whole area. Dean Heath at the eastern end of Dean Wood belonged to Amesbury Manor in 1540 (App.IV) and in 1740[21] but it did not appear in the 1726 survey of the wood[13]. In 1868 Howe Farm and 168 acres of woodland were acquired from St. Nicholas' Hospital by Thomas Baring of Norman Court in exchange for land on the outskirts of Salisbury[23].

28

Fig 12a *Details of Fig 12, Dean Wood circa 1800. (WCRO ref 727/13/10)*
(M Baskerville)

We can get some idea of what the land would have looked like in the mid 19th century from the 1843 West Dean tithe map, and from the 1874 OS map. By that time much of what had previously been rough grazing had become coppiced woodland. The old name Dean Heath had disappeared by 1844, when the tithe award was granted. Beechwood and Bushey Coppices were still called "commons", although they were classed as woodland in the award. By 1874 they had been renamed, Bushey Common had become Elm's Copse, and Beechwood was now called a copse.

The Southern Part of the Wood

In 1086, when the Domesday Book was compiled, West Dean manor belonged to Waleran, William the Conqueror's huntsman. He held the manor himself, it was not leased out as were some of his other estates in the district. The area of woodland which was attached to West Dean at that time was not very great; according to the Domesday Book it measured "1 furlong in both length and width " but there is, of course, no indication of its whereabouts. The small patches of woodland such as Fine Wood, which may have been slightly larger than in modern times, probably account for it. Waleran also held Grimstead, Whaddon and Norman Court manors among his other holdings, but these were leased out. He was the first Warden of the New Forest, a hereditary post of considerable importance. At that time Clarendon and Bentley were included in the New Forest bailiwick.

West Dean manor and the Wardenship continued to be held by the Waleran family until Walter Walerand died in about 1200 leaving three daughters, Cecilia, Albrede and Isabel. The estate, which also included the manor of East Grimstead, was then divided between the three girls. Isabel, the wife of Walter Walerand and the girls' mother, was related to Ela Longespee, Countess of Salisbury, and Ela gave part of the southern end of Bentley Wood to the husbands of the three sisters in 1227, following the death of her husband, William Longespee[14]. From that time onwards West Dean manor included the southern fringe of Bentley Wood (Fig.5).

One daughter, Cecilia, died without an heir so the estate continued to follow the descent of the remaining two sisters. Several generations later both halves of the manor were re-united by marriage, and were sold to Henry Gifford around 1577-79, so that it was once more a single estate[20].

In 1618 the Evelyn family bought the manor. George Evelyn had made a fortune selling gunpowder and his son John erected an imposing mansion house, Dean House. It stood in a grove of elm trees near the parish church and had elaborate formal gardens. There was also parkland with canals and a fishpond fed with water from the adjoining river Dun. The 14th century de Borbach Chantry, a mortuary chapel in the village graveyard, contains an elaborate monument to Sir John Evelyn and his family[21].

John Evelyn was a staunch supporter of the Roundhead cause in the Civil War. In 1644 a troop of the Roundhead army made their way to Southampton with 80 prisoners which they had taken while defeating the Cavaliers in Salisbury. They went by way of Dean House, where they were welcomed and provided with particularly good quarters. During the Civil War the south Wiltshire and Hampshire border area saw frequent skirmishes between the two sides, with troops passing through, sometimes taking prisoners and horses from the local communities as they went (Fig.13). An 8 pound cannon ball was found buried in a West Dean farmyard[21]. Bentley Wood was probably not affected directly, although the Civil War was generally very disruptive of normal working life for the villagers, and much damage was done throughout Wessex by both sides.

Fig 13 *A civil war soldier (R Pearce)*

A notable resident of West Dean during the 1750s was the naturalist Gilbert White, author of The Natural History of Selborne. He was curate there for a time but unfortunately did not become rector; a more prolonged stay might have produced a Natural History of Bentley Wood[22].

In 1781, for a second time in its history, West Dean manor was again divided up, this time following the death of Arthur, Lord Ranelagh and his wife. It remained within the family, divided between the descendants of Lord

Fig 14 *West Dean House (Colt Hoare vol. 5)*
(photo A Baskerville)

Ranelagh's sisters. All parts of the estate were finally sold to Charles Baring Wall of Norman Court in 1820, and the splendid manor house (Fig. 14), now in a very poor state of repair, was pulled down[21].

Norman Court

The ownership of Bentley Wood, from the Norman Conquest onwards, has now almost been accounted for. However, there are a few small, but not insignificant, areas left over.

On the east side of the wood, Park Copse lay within a detached portion of Winterslow, and although there was only a broad track between, was separate from the rest of the wood. This land belonged to Norman Court (Fig.5). The manor was held by Waleran the Huntsman in the Domesday Book but it was leased to a tenant, and was not connected to his West Dean estate. The name, Norman Court, came later, when it was bought by Roger de Norman. He acquired the West Bailey of Buckholt in 1334 from Steven de Loveras, the last Master of the King's Wolfhounds, and with this went the manor in West

Tytherley. More recent owners included the Whit(e)head and Thistlethwaite families. The Whit(e)heads were lords of the manor from the 16th century followed by the Thistlethwaite family from Winterslow. Charles Wall bought the manor from the Thistlethwaites in the early 19th century and he was succeeded by his son, Charles Baring Wall, in 1816. Throughout all this time Park Copse was the only part of Bentley Wood belonging to Norman Court. During the 19th century the other parts of the wood were gradually purchased and added to the Norman Court estate. In 1820 Baring Wall bought West Dean Manor, with which he acquired the southern part of the wood. After the Amesbury estate was sold in 1825 he bought the northern half. In 1853 Charles Baring Wall died and was succeeded by his mother's nephew, Thomas Baring, MP for Huntingdon and head of the Baring bank enterprises. Baring acquired the Howe Farm part of Bentley Wood in 1868, thus bringing together most of the wood into one ownership[23].

The final missing piece of the jigsaw was Richwellstead Copse. Richwellstead is part of the parish of Winterslow, unlike the rest of the wood, which is in the parish of West Dean. The parish boundary follows the coppice boundary bank, which is still just about visible, through the wood until it meets one of the tracks which then forms the boundary. This parish boundary is a good indication that the separation is a very old one. Richwellstead belonged to the manor of East Winterslow from Anglo-Saxon times, and remained part of the subsequent Roche Court estate throughout the long history of Bentley Wood. Roche Court was sold in 1920 and Richwellstead went to Norman Court; the jigsaw was finally complete.

4

Bentley in Clarendon Forest

Following the Norman Conquest the development of the countryside in South Wiltshire was dominated by the creation of extensive royal hunting forests. These were large areas of land which the Norman and Plantagenet kings designated as subject to forest laws. This protected game species, particularly deer, within the designated area, and also the "vert", or trees and undergrowth which provided food for the deer to eat. A forest in medieval times was therefore an area of land to which Forest Law applied, regardless of who owned it or what it was used for.

Hunting was much more than just a sport of kings and noblemen. Originally it had been the pursuit of animals for food, which during Anglo-Saxon times had in addition become an exciting and challenging recreational activity. It also provided an opportunity for developing the techniques and weapons which were needed in battle, and for maintaining the necessary skills of warfare. The crossbow was introduced by the Normans, only to be superseded in the 13th century by the longbow.

At the time of William the Conqueror and the Domesday Book, Bentley Wood was part of a royal estate, but from the 1140s onwards, when Amesbury manor was given to the Earl of Salisbury, it was in private hands. Although the estate was no longer held by the king, it still remained within the royal forest of Clarendon, and Bentley Wood was subject to Forest Law.

Forests were usually developed in moderately wooded areas interspersed with heath or agricultural land and were mainly land of low population density but not necessarily large tracts of continuous woodland. The forests developed as an extension of the hunting grounds which the Anglo- Saxon kings had established within their own demesne lands. However, although the Norman forests had started on Crown land, often in the vicinity of a royal residence, by 1086 they had spread far into the surrounding countryside. This meant that although the king owned the deer in the forest, his subjects often held the land[1]. Afforestation, or the imposition of Forest Law on an area, reached its maximum extent under Henry II[2] in the 12th century.

Fig 15 *A fallow buck (R Pearce)*

The "beasts of the forest" which could only be hunted by the king, were deer, wild boar and wolves. Wolves were still present in Wiltshire at the time of the Norman Conquest and William the Conqueror's wolfhounds were kept at the Livery (Louveras, or wolfhound kennels) on the edge of Bentley Wood[3]. They also gave their name to Hound Wood. The wolf was hunted to extinction in Clarendon in the early 14th century. Wild boar were still plentiful in the 12th century and were present in small numbers, although not necessarily locally, until the 15th century. They were never completely exterminated as the last few were thought to have interbred with domestic pigs, which also roamed the woodland. Hunting and killing a wild boar was an act of considerable bravery and many men and dogs were injured in the process. The boar was pursued with dogs until it finally turned to attack, when it was slain by a huntsman at very close quarters with a sword or spear. Not surprisingly the boar's head was a much–prized trophy and was served at ceremonial meals.

The deer were mainly fallow deer, which had been introduced, or reintroduced, by the Normans, but there were also the indigenous red and roe deer. Although deer hunting was sport for the king and his courtiers, the capture of the deer was often carried out by professional huntsmen to provide meat for royal feasts or when the king wanted to reward his subjects with gifts of venison. It was an important source of meat, particularly in the winter.

All surplus domestic animals had to be killed in the autumn as the hay and corn supplies were not adequate to feed them through the winter, whereas deer provided for themselves. Deer hunting was carried out both on foot and on horseback. An early medieval hunt involved finding and driving the selected beast towards an enclosure or nets where it was shot with a bow and arrow or pulled down with dogs. Various "types" of dogs were used during the hunt for different purposes, and they were unleashed in small numbers at a time. The use of a large pack of dogs, of all the same breed, to find the deer and then to pursue it for many miles across country, was a much later development.

The royal forests which were created in the well-wooded south east corner of Wiltshire were originally all regarded as an extension of the New Forest. The area included the future Clarendon Forest, of which Bentley Wood was part, and the whole area was managed by the Warden of the New Forest. Bentley Wood was said to have been afforested by Henry II (1154-1189)[4]. In 1228 Henry III created a separate royal forest of Clarendon which included the land around the palace of Clarendon. Clarendon then became the centre from which Buckholt, Melchet, Grovely and Clarendon were administered.

Administration of the royal forests, which principally involved upholding the forest laws, was carried out by the Warden and the Foresters. The Wardenship was a prestigious royal appointment and the land under his control was known as his bailiwick. The post was hereditary under the Norman kings and in the New Forest and Clarendon the post was first held by Waleran, William I's huntsman, and then by his descendants[4]. Waleran had his stronghold at West Dean on the edge of Bentley Wood, and the Walerand family became the early holders of West Dean manor. Under the Warden were the Foresters. The principal Foresters were the Foresters-of-fee, who were in charge of subdivisions of the forest, and they also held their position as a hereditary right.

Up to the 14th century Wardens and Foresters-in-fee had to pay a farm (annual fee) to hold their bailiwicks, but the perks which came with the job were considerable. As well as providing themselves with wood for building construction and grazing rights for their animals, Wardens kept the fines taken in their role of overseeing the forest laws, and the tolls levied on people passing through the forest[4]. In 1355 the Warden of Clarendon's perquisites included all stray animals which had been impounded and were unclaimed after a year and a day[4].

Where woodland within a royal forest was held by a subject, a woodward had to be appointed whose duties were similar to those of a forester. Woodwards were subordinate to foresters and could not carry bows and arrows in the woods, only billhooks and hatchets.

Grant during pleasure to Richard Etton, the king's serjeant of the office of Wodewardship of Bentilwode and Erles Milchet co Wilts, which belonged to the late earl of Salisbury and afterwards by gift to John, late Duke of Bedford; to hold himself or by deputy, with the accustomed wages, fees and profits. (Calendar of Patent Rolls. 1437)

Transgressions against Forest Law and other complaints were heard before the king's judges at the forest eyres (courts). The king's justices began visiting Wiltshire from the reign of Henry I onwards. Later in the 12th century Henry II developed a justice system whereby itinerant judges were sent to all parts of the country where they formed a court with a jury of local knights. The forest eyres were organised in a similar way with two judges appointed to a circuit covering all royal forests south of the Trent. The time interval between eyres was very variable, often only once every several years. In the 13th century the courts were held in Wilton but later courts took place in Salisbury. Offences brought before the court included taking deer or cutting down more than a specified amount of wood. Cutting down woodland was termed waste; if the roots were removed to make agricultural land, it was an assart. Originally, Norman Forest Law was very harsh and attempting to capture a deer was punishable by death. The king was not just protecting his sporting and recreational rights, venison was an important part of the wealth of the Crown and used as currency to pay for goods or services rendered. Over the succeeding centuries punishment became less severe.

During the 14th century triennial inquiries were held, known as the Regard, or an "inquiry regarding the condition of the forest". Forest wardens, Foresters and Regarders investigated offences against Forest Law. The Regard was held at rather irregular intervals, and during the 13th century it was often held shortly before a forest eyre and the offenders were then brought before the justices at the eyre. Being a Regarder was an unpaid office held by knights in the area and in the 13th century there were twelve regarders for the group of forests which included Clarendon and Bentley Wood[4]. By this time punishing offences against Forest Law was in fact considered much less important than raising Crown revenue from the fines imposed. Although the land was seized when an assart, or illegal clearing, was reported, it was usually handed back when a fee had

Fig 16 *The bounds of Clarendon Forest in 1327 shown on the OS Landranger 184 map, 1988. Crown copyright. All rights reserved. Licence no. WL8103.*

Fig 17 *The remains of old wood banks in Bentley Wood. (A Baskerville)*

Fig 18 *Hunting deer (R Pearce)*

been paid and an annual rent set[9]. Minor offences were heard at the local forest court. Once a fine had been paid at the forest eyre, cultivation was permitted and the land could be enclosed with a low bank and hedge "according to the standards of the forest and in such a manner that deer and fawns could enter and return"[5].

The royal hunting forests were very unpopular, particularly when Henry II and his sons Richard I and John expanded the areas to which Forest Law applied. Agriculture was difficult, since afforested land could not be cleared properly and cultivated areas could not be enclosed by hedges to prevent deer eating the crops. However, the struggle to get these areas disafforested has to be seen in the context of the time. During the medieval period there was a constant battle for power between the Plantagenet kings and the barons. The distribution of land in England after the Conquest was fundamentally different from the organisation of land ownership in either Anglo-Saxon England or in Normandy. No subject owned land, it all belonged to the king. Large estates were then "held" by tenants-in-chief, or barons, in return for services given or promised. On the death of the tenant-in-chief the land escheated (reverted back) to the

Crown. In the same way parcels of land were then subinfeudated (sub-let) by the barons and formed the basis of the feudal system[6]. This system gave the king a hold over his most powerful subjects but the lack of hereditary rights caused considerable unrest. Another cause of constant discontent was the frequent demands made by the king for money from the barons to finance various wars and crusades.

The struggle against Forest Law was therefore just one of a number of reasons for long running discontent and outright rebellion. When Magna Carta, or a charter of liberties, was forced on King John in 1215 it contained three clauses about the forest bounds. The charter was reissued in 1217 with the clauses relating to royal forests withdrawn and these were then expanded and issued as a separate Forest Charter[7].

The Forest Charter was issued again in 1225 by HenryIII with the forest bounds set to where they had been at the beginning of HenryII's reign (1154). A perambulation of Clarendon Forest (an inspection of the perimeter) was carried out by the knights to set their rightful bounds, and this perambulation disafforested Bentley Wood. Odo of Grimstead's wood (Hawksgrove Copse in Bentley Wood) was to be "exempt the Regard", or not subject to inspection by the Regarders. However, the king, Henry III, forced the knights to agree to his claim for wider bounds than they had allowed[4]. The Forest Charter also limited the harsh treatment of the people of the forest by the foresters and the punishments for breach of Forest Law were greatly reduced. "No man should lose life or limb for hunting deer." Only the senior foresters, the foresters–in–fee, could exact tolls for carts passing through the forest, and then only if they were transporting wood for sale; there was to be no charge when a man was carrying the wood on his back. It was still to be an offence to have a mastiff or large dog anywhere in the forest unless it had been "lawed", which was the removal of three toes on a forefoot, but the penalty was to be a fine of 3 shillings rather than the customary seizure of the owner's ox[5].

In 1299 Edward I confirmed the Charter of Henry III, but omitted the clauses of the Forest Charter about disafforestation of earlier encroachments[8]. In 1300 the Charters were confirmed, this time with the Charter of Forests in full. However in 1305 Edward I reduced the effects of a perambulation carried out at that time by denying to persons who lived outside the new bounds of the forest the rights of pasture within the bounds. In 1306 he annulled the disafforestations altogether[8]. A later perambulation gives the forest boundaries as they were in 1327 (Fig.16) and Bentley, Prior's wood (Prior's copse) and Archer's wood (possibly Hatcher's copse, or more likely, Barnridge) were still "within the regard"[4].

After Henry III royal interest in the forests as game reserves gradually declined, especially in areas outside royal demesne land and from about the middle of the 14th century forest laws and institutions were of little account[4].

Woodland during the medieval period, regardless of whether it was in a royal forest or not, was managed as a much valued renewable resource and the demand for woodland products at that time was very high[2]. The bulk of the wood was produced by coppicing and pollarding the underwood on a continuous cycle of around 7-10 years. This produced small diameter lengths of wood for fuel, charcoal, wattle for buildings, fences and hurdles. Hazel was particularly common for wattle and can still be found hidden in the walls of old buildings[9]. Timber from mature trees, particularly oak for large structural timbers in buildings, was only cut when required, since it obviously took a long time to regenerate.

Both timber and underwood from royal forests were given as gifts to influential subjects and particularly to the church; mature timber represented a major financial grant from the sovereign. The new Salisbury Cathedral and the town surrounding it, together with the enlargements to the palace at Clarendon would have been a considerable drain on the surrounding royal forests during the 13th century.

From the reign of Edward I the Rolls (royal records) contain orders to the Wardens of Clarendon, Bentley and Pancet to inspect underwood and sell small acreages where it would provide least damage to game and woodland[10].

1429 Commission to John Pruet to cut down underwood and oak trees in Bentley wood and sell the same for the king's best avail (Calendar of Patent Rolls 1429-36).

Wood and timber were regularly taken from the forests as royal gifts and to raise revenue for the Crown; the king was expected to finance himself to a large extent from his own estates. Wood was also taken by the foresters as part of their rights. Some was taken illegally and, in addition, the woodland areas were steadily reduced by assarts or the illegal clearing and ploughing up of woodland.

Efforts were made from time to time to redress the balance, and to prevent timber supplies in the country from becoming too depleted. In 1482 Edward IV brought in an Act for Inclosing of Woods in Forests, Chases and Purlieus. Hitherto owners of woodland had only been allowed to enclose their coppices for three years after cutting, to ensure adequate "vert" for the deer. Henceforth they could fence them for seven years to prevent damage by browsing animals, both wild and domestic. This act therefore eased some of the hardship caused to woodland owners by the previous forest laws.

The 1540 Rent Roll of Edward Seymour (App. IV) gives the acreages of some of the coppices in Bentley Wood. The figures are considerably smaller than those recorded in the 19th century and probably represent the areas which were actually enclosed (see table 1).

Table 1.

A Comparison of Copse Sizes given in (1) The Rent Roll of Edward Seymour 1540, (2) The 1813 Valuation of Bentley Wood for Amesbury Estate and (3) The West Dean Tithe Map 1843. Areas given in Acres.

	1540	1813	1843
Coalpits	30	48	48
Redman's Gore	20	50	50
Picked	30	62	62
Priors	20	61	61
Mapleway Dean	21	52	52
Hooping Oak	30	59	59
3 Sisters+Smokeways	50	107	107
Armitage	20	49	49

The 1813 area often includes the lane adjoining.

In 1543 Henry VIII was sufficiently concerned about the lack of timber that he introduced an Act for the Preservation of Woodland because:

"there is a great and manifest likelihood of scarcity and lack of timber for building, making and repairing and maintaining of houses and ships, and also for fewel and firewood".

When coppice woods or underwoods were cut at 24 years growth or less, 12 oak trees per acre were to be left to grow on to produce timber trees. If there were not enough oak trees, then elm, ash, aspen or beech had to be left instead. These could not be felled until they were all at least 10 inches square within 3 feet of the ground[11].

The problem of inadequate timber supplies was a constantly recurring one, and parliament was still trying to resolve it in later centuries when naval and merchant shipping enterprises needed more, and bigger, wooden ships.

5

The Medieval Woodland

We now know who owned Bentley Wood during medieval and later times, but can we get any impression of what the landscape looked like during the many centuries that followed the Norman Conquest? There are not the detailed maps and records of woodland usage that are available for the 18th and 19th centuries, but we can form at least some idea of the nature and extent of the wood in those times.

Unfortunately we get no help from the Domesday survey of 1086, as Bentley Wood was not recorded individually, it was just part of the 29,000 acres of woodland belonging to the royal manor of Amesbury. Bentley Wood, or Bentilwode, was known by name, and exists in the records, by the 13th century, which implies that it was an identifiable stretch of woodland at that time, and probably much earlier.

The modern familiar outline of the wood is first recognizable on the 18th and early 19th century maps of Wiltshire, even though such maps do not give much detail and are not very accurate. However, some of the boundaries which form this outline are likely to be very old, particularly where they are parish boundaries. Such boundaries are mainly Anglo-Saxon in origin, representing the dividing line between estates. The western edge of the wood, which follows the bridle path from Witt road, Winterslow, to the Livery, Farley, is the boundary between West Dean and Winterslow parishes. Any woodland on the Winterslow side of the boundary was in the ownership of Winterslow manor. In the 14th century the manor was held by Idonea de Leybourne and at the Inquisition Post Mortem[1] following her death in 1334 it included

300 acres of wood lying in the forest of Claryndone.

This 300 acres would have included Houndwood, Chickard Wood and some unidentified woodland between Bentley and Hound woods. A perambulation of Penchet Forest (part of Clarendon) in the time of Henry III (1216-1272) gives as landmarks;

By the ditch into Bentlewode

By the bounds between Bentlewode and Hundewode

This has been interpreted as meaning that Houndwood extended across to Bentley in the neighbourhood of Livery Farm[2]. We can therefore assume that there were probably areas of woodland on the western side of Bentley Wood, owned by a different estate and varying in extent over the centuries.

Continuing this boundary further south, the woodland would have merged with the partially wooded common lands of Farley and Grimstead, forming Cook's Common and the Marsh for example. In medieval times the extensive ancient commons formed a continuous area of wet land from Farley to Hawksgrove and up to the Livery, including White's Common and Blackmore[3]. Barnridge was probably originally similar rough pasture with a variable amount of scrub and tree cover. On the eastern side of the wood there is again a parish boundary, the boundary between West Dean and a detached portion of Winterslow. The division ran through the wood, along Park Lane, between Park Copse and the rest of the wood. There may well at some stage have been woodland or wood pasture across the adjacent fields belonging to Norman Court.

The southern border of the wood is typical of woodland which has been eroded by assarts, which were areas cleared of trees and scrub to make pasture or arable land. This creates a jagged outline of individual fields pushing into the woodland, unlike the smooth curve of old estate boundaries. There is nothing to indicate in which century this may have happened around the south eastern boundary. Further west, following the southern border, the assart of William Longespee in the early 13th century created the deep indentation of the Howe Farm fields. The fields along the road from West Dean to West Tytherley, which are adjacent to Bentley Wood, had names in the 19th century such as North and South Common, Rail Common and Bushy Common, which suggest a broad band of common grazing lying outside the wood boundary and joining up with Tytherley Common.

To gain an impression of the appearance of the land within the bounds of the wood we must consider the nature of English woodland in general during the medieval period. Timber and wood could be harvested either from managed woodland, or from pollarded trees on common grazing land, as well as a significant quantity from the hedgerows. Managed coppices maximized wood production, and were therefore the system favoured by landowners; wood

Fig 19 *Charcoal burners. (R Pearce)*

pasture allowed grazing for commoners' animals without any disruption following cutting[4]. Since wood was the main reason why the landlords of Amesbury manor retained the northern half of Bentley Wood, the majority of their woodland was likely to have been managed to provide as much as possible. Amesbury Priory was also taking a daily cartload.

The medieval requirement for woodland products was on a vast scale, as we have already mentioned (Bentley in Clarendon Forest). There was a general increase in population during the 13th century which led to the erosion of many woodland areas for arable and pasture land, but must also have increased the requirements for wood as fuel and building material. A large part of the wood was therefore likely to have been managed as coppice with standards, the underwood being cut at variable intervals depending on the local conditions at the time. Following the Norman Conquest owners of woodland were, of course, severely restricted by forest laws, which prevented them from taking large quantities of their own wood, or from adequately fencing newly cut coppice to help regeneration. As the interest in maintaining large forest areas for hunting declined, the emphasis changed to encouraging and preserving the growth of underwood and timber. However, there were also areas of wood-pasture since the viability of rural communities relied on some provision for grazing animals.

Coppiced woods required protective banks with hedges on top to keep out browsing animals, which would damage the new growth. Some of the banks are still clearly visible in Bentley Wood (Fig.17), although much reduced in size, and many are likely to be medieval in origin. Rackham[5] states that the typical structure is a large bank, usually rounded, with an external ditch and that where the bank turns a sharp corner there is a corner mound. On top of the bank there would have been a hedge. The vestiges of old banks which can still be seen in Bentley Wood are principally round the wood edge, or where there is a change of ownership. The banks which define the southern boundary of the land which belonged to Amesbury Manor are still very pronounced today. In the late 16th century, when relations between the various owners and woodland workers were particularly bad, the bank and ditch along the east side of Rowley Marsh were created (see Fig. 20) which prevented access to the woodland grazing[11,12]. Individual copses probably had wooden woven fences to keep farm animals out for a few years after cutting. Woodland records of the 16th and 17th centuries give some indication of what the wood would have looked like at that time. Table I in chapter 4 shows that there were probably fenced areas of coppice within more open woodland. It is known that St. Nicholas' Hospital and Howe Farm had common grazing rights throughout the wood so that for part of the year at least there would have been cattle and sheep feeding between the fenced-in coppices.

The underwood was cut on a regular basis, although the length of time which it was allowed to grow varied considerably. Owners of woodland frequently had little regard for the long-term management, which, coupled with urgent requirements for timber, often led to excessive cutting of standard trees. The result must have been some very bare-looking areas at times.

Records of the forest eyres when Bentley Wood was still subject to Forest Law provide some evidence to suggest that the northern part of the wood was sometimes cropped rather heavily, the errant owners having to pay the customary fine of $\frac{1}{2}$ mark unless they were the nuns, who were exempt payment by royal charter[6].

Eyre 1262-3 Matil' Lungespye de Bentilwud waste of wood $\frac{1}{2}$ mark.

Fig 20 *Rowley Marsh (Barnridge Meadow) with its boundary bank. (A Baskerville)*

Eyre 1330 John de Warenne, Earl of Surrey, for waste in his wood Bentelwode ½ mark.

When Henry de Lacy, Earl of Lincoln, was lord of the manor of Amesbury and was called to account for waste in Bentley Wood, it was noted that the Prioress of Amesbury was allowed a daily cartload of wood by royal charter, and there was therefore no fine[7].

The 14th century saw a dramatic reduction in the population in this country. The overpopulation of the previous century had only been sustained by using every possible area of land for growing crops, including difficult and marginal land. A series of harvest failures led to famine in the early 14th century, followed by epidemics of the Black Death, which started in 1348. The population of England was reduced by a third to a half and villages became deserted, or shrank in size and land was no longer cultivated. Landlords could not get the labour they needed to run their own agricultural enterprises and took to leasing their land. As the countryside gradually recovered there was a shift to pastoral farming, which was less labour-intensive, and the products, wool, meat and milk were still profitable[8]. We have no direct evidence, but such profound changes must have affected Bentley Wood. With a drop in the local population for two or three generations the underwood would have regenerated relatively undisturbed for a long period, the higher canopy increased and scrub invaded the open pasture. However, impoverished landlords often had to try and sell their assets, and some timber may therefore have been felled when conditions allowed.

As we get nearer to more recent times there are more records and the picture becomes clearer. Although much of the wood was coppiced woodland, there were some areas which were rough grazing or wood pasture. The Marsh, or Rowley Marsh (Fig.20) appears to have been wet grazing land for a long time and would have looked much the same as it does today under the modern name of Barnridge Meadow. Dean Heath was on the south-eastern side of the wood and was probably open heathland with pollarded oaks and a variable amount of scrub. There are records from the early 17th century of pollards being "shrouded" or cut[11]. Berryfield and Donkey copse were all woodland by the 1837 tithe award but the names suggest that they too were previously open land.

It is likely that the predominant tree species present during the Middle Ages would have been similar to those during the 18th and 19th centuries, for which we have rather more firm information. The requirements for wood products would have been the same throughout, with additional demands from time to time. The need for hazel hurdles for animal enclosures and fences would always have been considerable. In the days before bricks were commonly used, many houses would have been timber framed with wattle and daub infilling. Hazel was used for the wattle and oak was the commonest and most sought-after building timber[5]. We can therefore be fairly certain that these species would have been encouraged in the woodland. Coppicing the hazel ensured that individual stools survived for long periods of time, and there would have been new saplings growing up, eventually to replace them. The oak trees were allowed to grow until they reached the size required for building timber. A few large ash are recorded in tree surveys at a later date and ash was probably coppiced as part of the "underwood". There were also individual yew trees. Willow and alder would have grown in the damper places and a few of the coppice names suggest the presence of other species, particularly Beechways and Mapleway Dean. The maple was the field maple. Areas of thorn and bramble would have provided shelter for the grazing animals on the open areas, which when cut down and piled together made a useful temporary fence. Plantations were very rare before the 17th century[9] and we have no evidence of any in Bentley Wood before the 20th century.

A woodsman from the 19th century would have recognized much of what he saw if he had been walking through the wood a few hundred years earlier, the landscape was broadly similar. He would also have recognized the working scene, both the main tasks of cutting and carting wood and the rural industries which were all part of the woodland economy. He would have seen hurdle makers in the newly-cut coppices, stacks of wood being loaded onto carts for the journey to Amesbury and smoke from the charcoal burners gently drifting upwards (Fig.19). At some very early date charcoal was probably produced in pits in Coalpits Copse. Later, when it was made in mounds above ground, there would have been burning sites in different places at different times. It is known that St. Nicholas' Hospital had an annual cartload of charcoal from the Howe Farm area. The woodland floor would have looked very clean and tidy as small ends of wood and broken branches represented valuable firewood to the local workforce. The regular opening up of coppice areas when they were cut, and the periodic felling of timber trees would have allowed the ground flora to flourish in a cyclical way.

The domestic cattle grazing on the rough pasture areas would have been a mixed bunch, of rather diverse ancestry. Originally, when used almost exclusively for draught, they would have been strong, big-bodied animals, with the very long horns seen today in Longhorn or Highland cattle. Later the red-coated medium-horned beasts, which the Saxons had originally imported, also became common. They acted as the medieval farmer's tractor, pulling the plough and hauling wood, as well as providing meat and milk. The lightly built Channel Island cattle, with their rich milk, were found in southernmost counties and may sometimes have had an influence on local cattle breeding[10]. However, there were no fixed breeds and a mixture of all types could be represented.

During the early medieval period there would not have been any sheep or goats around the woodland; they were forbidden by law from grazing in Forest areas because their feeding habits were too similar to those of the deer and they would compete for the "vert". When the Norman forest laws no longer applied there were likely to have been at least some sheep in the wood, particularly as one of the common grazing areas was called Ramshill. Pigs were particularly well suited to the woodland environment, and in pannage time there could have been quite large numbers feeding around the wood.

The time period which we have been considering is a long one, and there were many factors which would have affected life in the woodland from time to time. We have already noted the population changes, the formation of royal forests and their gradual demise, and the effects of civil war. There were occasional devastating storms. Great gales resulting in large numbers of wind-fallen trees occurred in Clarendon and Buckholt forests in 1223 and 1368 and it is unlikely that Bentley Wood would have escaped without similar damage. Climatic changes were also known to have occurred, particularly during the little Ice Age. For about two centuries from the 1490s there were cold winters, with prolonged frost and snow, and cool wet summers. Although such conditions would have had less dramatic effects on trees than on annual agricultural crops, it must have made life very hard for the villagers working in the woodland. Hauling the wood over the hills to Amesbury during particularly hard winters must have been even more of a struggle than usual.

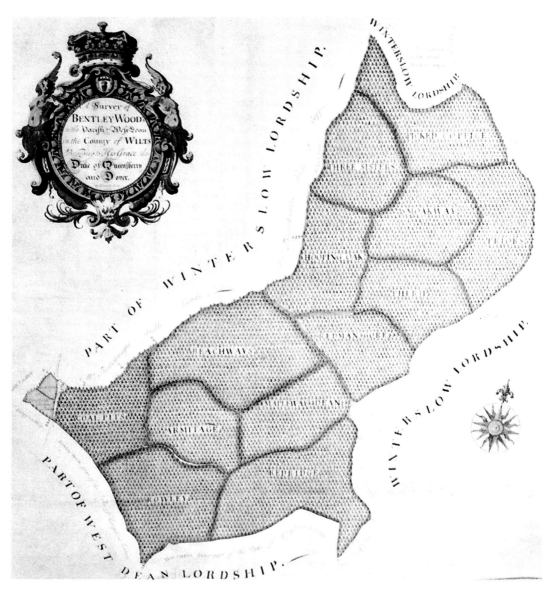

Fig 21 *An estate map, 1726, showing the part of Bentley Wood which belonged to Amesbury manor (WCRO ref 994/1-2). (photo A Baskerville)*

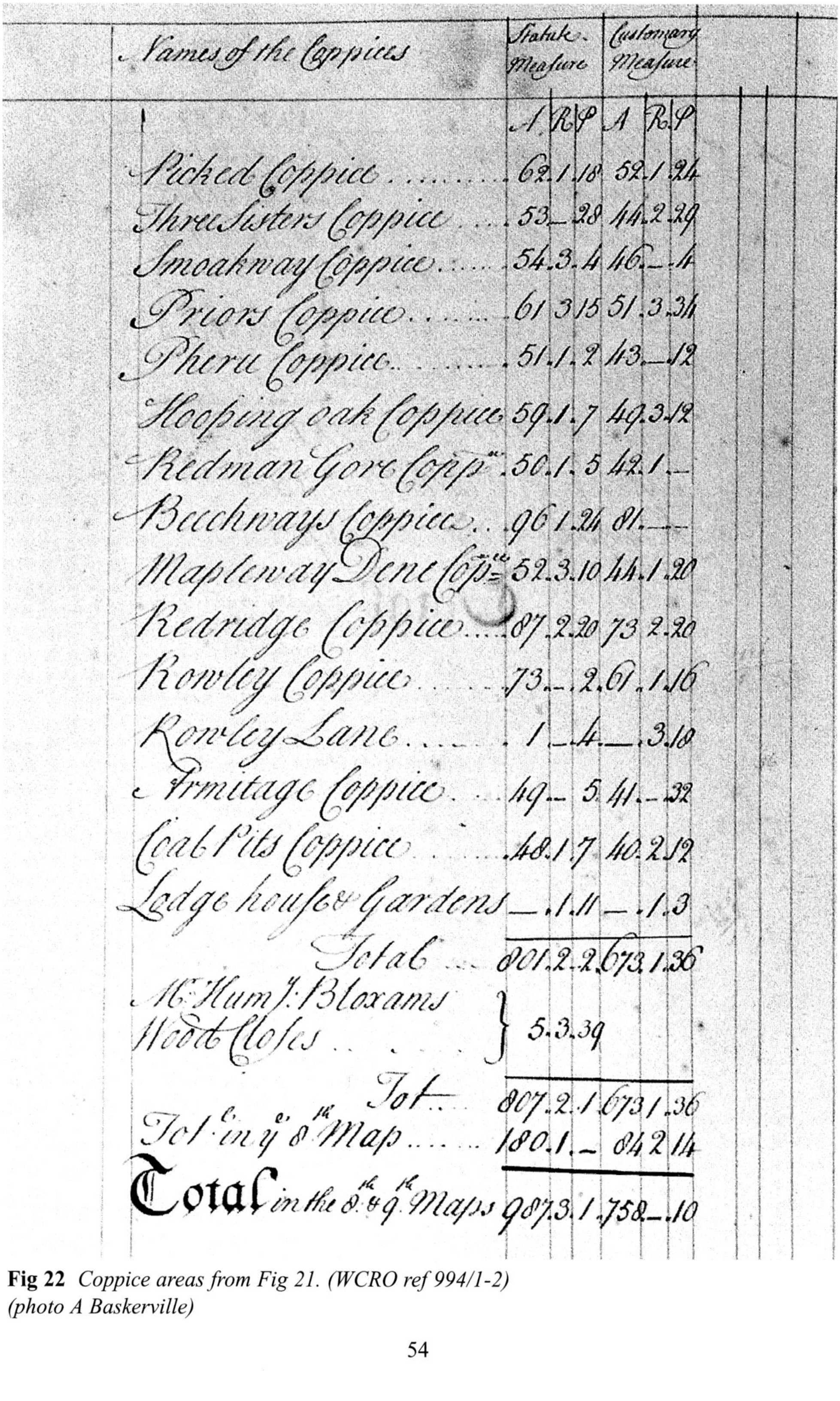

Names of the Coppices	Statute Measure			Customary Measure		
	A	R	P	A	R	P
Picked Coppice	62	1	18	52	1	24
Three Sisters Coppice	53	—	28	44	2	29
Smoakway Coppice	54	3	4	46	—	4
Priors Coppice	61	3	15	51	3	34
Pheru Coppice	51	1	2	43	—	12
Hooping oak Coppice	59	1	7	49	3	12
Redman Gore Copp.	50	1	5	42	1	—
Beechways Coppice	96	1	24	81	—	—
Mapleway Dene Cop.	52	3	10	44	1	20
Redridge Coppice	87	2	20	73	2	20
Rowley Coppice	73	—	2	61	1	16
Rowley Lane	1	—	4	—	3	18
Armitage Coppice	49	—	5	41	—	32
Coal Pits Coppice	48	1	7	40	2	12
Lodge house & Gardens	—	1	11	—	1	3
Total	801	2	2	673	1	36
Mr Hum J. Bloxams Wood Closes	5	3	39			
Tot.	807	2	1	673	1	36
Tot. in ye 8th Map	180	1	—	84	2	14
Total in the 8th & 9th Maps	987	3	1	758	—	10

Fig 22 *Coppice areas from Fig 21. (WCRO ref 994/1-2)*
(photo A Baskerville)

6

The 18th and 19th Centuries

The transition between the 17th and 18th centuries was not an abrupt one; woodlands continued to be managed in much the same way as they had been down through the ages since the Norman Conquest. However, there were some profound changes to life in Britain during the 18th and 19th centuries, such as the Industrial Revolution, which inevitably affected the use of wood and the management of woodland.

Maps and Records

From the 18th century onwards the countryside was described in increasingly informative documents and maps, and many of these records have survived and are available today. We have a much more detailed picture of Bentley Wood during the 18th and 19th centuries than we can get from previous times and it is easier to see how national trends affected our particular area of woodland.

County maps were produced in the 17th century, but they were very small and showed little detail apart from towns, rivers and the main through roads. Larger county maps of Wiltshire first appeared in the late 18th century, beginning with the Andrews and Dury map of 1773 at a scale of 2ins. to 1mile, which was based on an original survey (Fig.25). The early county maps were not always very accurate and often put undue emphasis on the gardens and orchards of large manor houses, whose owners were likely to buy the maps. However, these maps from the late 18th and early 19th centuries, several of which can be seen collected together, albeit on a rather small scale, in John Chandler's Printed Maps of Wiltshire 1787-1844[1], do at least show the outline of Bentley Wood, the surrounding villages and the principal roads and tracks. Unfortunately the maps were produced on a county basis, which is a disadvantage when looking at an area immediately adjacent to the county boundary. County maps produced by local cartographers were quickly superseded by the Old Series Ordnance Survey maps in the early 19th century. In the Old Series maps Bentley Wood is still shown as a block of trees.

In the late 19th century the Ordnance Survey produced their first modern, properly-surveyed, detailed maps of all regions of the country. The survey of 1874 resulted in the earliest really accurate large-scale maps which included the whole area in and around Bentley Wood. In contrast to the earlier maps, one can see in the 1874 edition at 25inches/mile such features as the coppices, and accurate figures for their areas and boundaries, and also the main woodland tracks and streams. The difference between coniferous, deciduous and mixed woodland is indicated, and areas of rough pasture are shown. These maps also cross the county boundary, although the survey dates for Wiltshire and Hampshire differ slightly.

Estate maps and surveys are another useful source of information. The 1726 map from the bound collection of maps of Amesbury estate (Fig.21) is not only a beautiful picture of the northern part of Bentley Wood, but quite a lot of information about the wood can be gleaned from it[2]. The map shows how much of the wood belonged to Amesbury, and the overall shape of the wood as shown is accurate when compared with modern maps (Fig.1,5). It also gives the names of the coppices as they were in the 18th century and some tracks. An accompanying book gives the coppice areas and these two carefully- written comments:

The Lanes on the map are not the real extent or outbounds of the several Lanes but are the representation of the pathways that are worn by the Wagons in going to and from the woods, for the remaining parts of the Lanes overgrown with wood, as coppices are, and for that reason the Lanes are measured into the adjoining coppices as is here mentioned.

About 20 years since there was a Tryal at Law (concerning the Lane called Park Lane) betwixt the Lord Bruce then owner of Bentley Woods and Esq Whitehead Owner of the adjoining Woods (called Park Woods) and it was determined that each owner should cut the wood in the lane as far as the Horse path which is represented in the map.

The map of Dean Wood circa 1800[3] shows the Howe Farm estate, which included extensive areas of Bentley Wood. Cook's Common is shown as part of the estate, and Blackmore Hill was also included, as "free on lease".

Norman Court estate was surveyed in 1807 and the survey shows that Park Copse, the only part of Bentley Wood owned by the estate at that time, was divided into a number of smaller areas. It was all managed in hand rather than leased to a tenant, and most of it was coppice. Two small areas are just described

Fig 23 *Recently cut hazel coppice (A Baskerville)*

Fig 24 *A bowl-shaped pit in Bentley Wood (A Baskerville)*

as "wood", which were probably also coppice. There are some interesting pencil notes, such as "sold for coppice 1820", which were obviously added at a later date. The adjacent fields are all described as arable[4].

The earliest map of West Dean manor is an estate map thought to date from about 1820[5]. It was probably surveyed at the time that the manor, together with East Grimstead, passed to the Earl of Enniskillen in 1816[5]. Dates of cutting are given for many of the coppices as a later addition, which adds to our knowledge of how the woodland was managed.

A very attractive 1781 estate map of Hancocks Farm (Farley Farm), which belonged to the Earl of Radnor, shows how the area around the Livery and Blackmoor Copse looked in the 18th century[6]. Much of the present Blackmoor Copse was arable land, and it also shows Blackmore Hill, the grazing land indicated on the Dean Wood map[3] as part of Bentley Wood. In 1836 the Tithe Commutation Act changed the age-old requirement for landowners, however small, to give a proportion of their produce each year to the rector of the parish. Woodland was included as titheable land and a proportion of the wood produced also had to be given to the church. An account from the St. Nicholas' Hospital papers gives the woodland tithe for the Howe Farm area of Bentley wood (Fig.5) in 1633 as 5 acres and 34 lugs[21]. For produce such as grain, hay and fruit, the tithe was traditionally a tenth of whatever was produced each year, but the requirements for woodland products were very variable in different regions. Tithes in woodland normally only applied to underwood and brushwood. By the 19th century many landowners made payments of money instead of produce. Under the Tithe Commutation Act a system of annual monetary payments to the rector of the parish completely replaced the giving in kind, and the amount given was standardised. The tithe was to be based on an average value of the crop in the country as a whole; the landowner then paid the agreed rate per acre for each crop.

To institute a fair tithe system the first requirement was for accurate, detailed maps of all the productive land in each parish. The result was the tithe maps and apportionments, most of which were drawn up around 1840, which give us so much information about the countryside in the mid-19th century. After much debate it was decided that the maps did not have to conform to a standard formula, but all parishes had to produce a detailed map and survey of the land, woodland as well as farmland[7].

The West Dean tithe map of 1843 gives the state of Bentley Wood at that time. The area of each coppice is recorded and most of the coppices are just described as "wood". Blackmore Hill was pasture and was included in the Howe

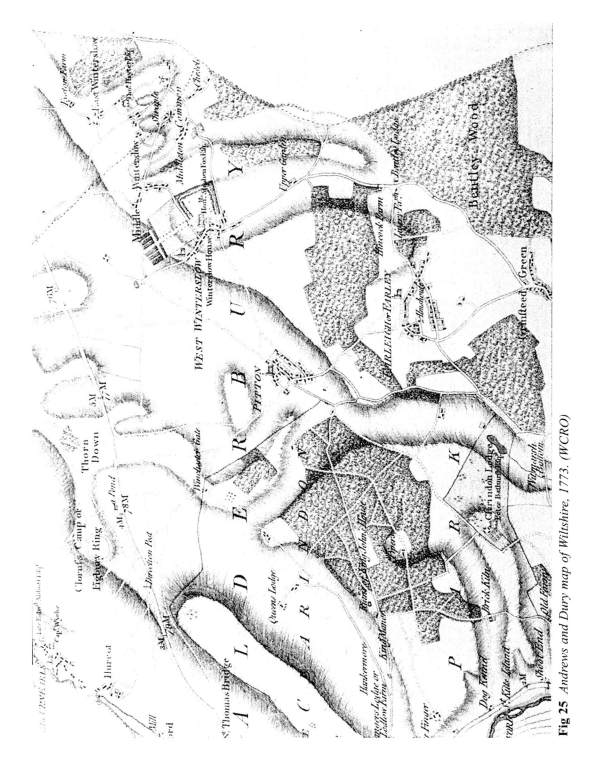

Fig 25 *Andrews and Dury map of Wiltshire, 1773. (WCRO)*

Farm estate, and Rowley Marsh was rough pasture. By 1843 much of the wood was owned by Charles Baring Wall and is given in the tithe apportionment under his name. The Howe Farm area of Bentley Wood was still separate and belonged to the Earl of Clarendon. The state of cultivation of all the fields in the parish of West Dean adjacent to Bentley Wood can also be seen, which gives a more complete picture of the area in general in the 1840s.

Richwellstead Copse is part of Winterslow parish and is therefore included in the 1841 Winterslow tithe map. One can see on the map the landscape around Witt road and the entrance to the wood. The main difference from today was an additional 100 acres of woodland adjacent to Bentley Wood, but separated from it by the track leading towards the Livery. Park Copse is also included in the Winterslow parish tithe apportionment and the coppice details are not significantly different from the 1807 Norman Court survey[4].

Agricultural Improvements

The 18th and 19th centuries were an era of fundamental changes and improvements in agriculture in Britain, and this affected the countryside as a whole, including the woodland.

One of the main changes was the enclosure of the old open fields, bringing to an end the feudal way of life in rural areas. Enclosure caused much hardship to the villagers involved, since they lost their rights of grazing on common land. It did, however, allow improvements in agriculture to take place which could not happen when crops and animals were in shared fields. Land which had previously been wet rough grazing land was drained with the newly-developed clay drainage tiles, which could now be made in industrial quantities. The Draining Field in Bentley Wood was treated in this way, and the old pipe tiles were present in the ground until recently.

Enclosure of the fields allowed individual farmers to improve the fertility of their soil, not only with farmyard manure or imported guano, but also by adding chalk or limestone to all fields apart from those where chalk was naturally part of the surface soil. Increasing numbers of small chalk pits appeared, often in the middle of the fields, where the underlying chalk was brought to the surface. Chalk was also dug out and carted from any other accessible piece of ground, particularly woodland (Fig. 24). Ellis's Husbandry in 1772[8] explains at length what was required:

The chalk drawer finds a wheel rope-barrow, and all other tackle, and sinks the pit for the price of eight pence a load, each load containing twenty wheel-barrows full, which they also for that money spread all about the field. Twenty five or thirty load will well chalk an acre of ground, Which by discreet ploughings will last twenty years.

Chalk had other uses, such as for building houses and barns, and to improve track surfaces, but the bulk of what was extracted was used to spread on fields. Many of the pits in Bentley wood are likely to have been the source of chalk for such purposes.

On the drained and fertilized land better crops could be grown, and the introduction of new varieties of cereals also improved the yields. Root crops, particularly turnips, were introduced and provided an invaluable source of animal food during the winter. The increased winter food production meant that large numbers of animals could be overwintered and there was no longer any need to kill and salt down all but essential breeding stock in the autumn. This in turn provided more manure for the fields. The greater numbers of farm animals in the countryside would have provided an increased market for woodland products, particularly hurdles, fences and gates.

Improvements in the breeding of farm animals also started in the 18th century, and herds of well-fed beef and dairy cattle, of recognizable modern breeds, would have appeared in the fields surrounding the woodland. The cottager's pig remained an essential part of the Victorian village economy, but the large herds of pigs which had roamed Bentley Wood in previous centuries were gradually replaced by cattle on the farms. A few animals would still have grazed the wet rough areas of poor pasture in the southern part of Bentley wood, but domestic livestock had really ceased to be part of the woodland scene. It was now the responsibility of farmers to put fences or hedges round their fields to keep their cattle in, rather than the custom of coppice owners to build a bank and ditch to keep them out. In 1797 a number of printed notices were produced by the agent for Amesbury estate on behalf of the owners of the northern and southern parts of the wood[24]:

WHEREAS the UNDERWOOD at Bentley and Dean, belonging to his Grace the Duke of Queensberry, and the Right Honourable the Earl of Clarendon, have of late years been much injured by Cattle, occasioned by the

Fences of the adjoining Grounds not being properly made; NOTICE IS HEREBY GIVEN, that if any Cattle are found in any of the said Underwoods after the Date hereof, an Action will be immediately commenced against the Owners of such Cattle for Damages.

Transport and the Industrial Revolution

Inevitably the industrial revolution and increasing mechanisation affected the lives of the labourers working in the woodland.

The gradual improvement in the quality of the surfaces of roads around the region would have made transport of wood, as well as the finished products from the coppice industries, easier, although country roads would still have been difficult in the winter months. Most of the wood and timber would have been used fairly locally, but easier transport allowed access to more distant markets when necessary. Completely new forms of transport, which revolutionised the movement of people and goods around Britain, started to be developed. The network of canals, which were dug in the 18th and early 19th centuries, allowed easy movement of heavy goods and coal could now literally flow around the country. This reduced the need for wood, which hitherto had been the only available fuel for both industrial and domestic use. The reduced demand allowed woodland to regenerate where it had previously been cut very heavily. Work on the Southampton to Salisbury canal commenced in 1795, with the aim of moving heavy goods inland to and from the port of Southampton. The proposed route of the canal ran from the Avon valley, through a tunnel at Alderbury, and along the Dean valley, just south of Bentley Wood, to join another canal at Kimbridge. Unfortunately the tunnel was never built, the scheme ran into financial difficulties and by 1808 the canal was abandoned. However, the section which ran through the Dean valley was finished and for a short time there was traffic on the canal between Dunbridge and West Dean where the wharf stood in front of the old Red Lion pub. Bentley Wood thus gained, and then lost, an easy route out not only for wood, but also for other heavy goods, such as chalk, and bricks from the brickworks on the edge of the wood.

The main reason for the excellent concept of water transport not fulfilling its obvious potential was the development of steam trains shortly afterwards, and the spread of the rail network was well advanced before the later canals were

Fig 26 *Horse-power in woodland. (B and J Davies)*

completed. The Salisbury to Southampton line was opened in 1847, which finally provided easy transport from West Dean for passengers and goods, to Southampton, London and the rest of Britain.

Despite the Industrial Revolution, work in the woodland and the coppice industries continued to be principally manual labour using hand tools. As with all major advances which reduce the manpower needed to carry out a task, the introduction of steam power into agriculture in the late 19th century was regarded as a threat rather than a benefit by the local workforce, and throughout the country many new threshing machines were destroyed by the rural workers. The old methods were intolerably hard by today's standards, but they represented employment and income to the Victorian village families. Woodland labourers probably regarded themselves as fortunate that coppice work and the felling of timber continued to be done by hand. However, the development of steam power did allow the mechanisation of some tasks. The circular saw, for example, powered by a steam engine, for cutting tree trunks into planks, was a great step forward, when compared with the classical saw-pit operated by two men with a hand saw. Although traction engines were eventually used to pull and transport timber (Fig.35), horse-power continued to be preferable under most conditions. Horses were manoeuvrable and could work in the wood without churning up the ground and tracks (Fig.26).

From the 17th century onwards the value of timber was considerably increased by its use in the expanding shipbuilding industry. The construction of naval vessels did not have a great effect on woodland, as the spreading oaks grown on wood pasture or in hedgerows were better suited in both size and shape. Merchant ship building, though, needed woodland-grown trees, and during the period 1700 to 1850 much of the available oak around Hampshire was depleted[9]. The Napoleonic wars at the beginning of the 19th century, and the global expansion of the British Empire, greatly increased the requirement for ships of all sizes, and created a heavy demand for timber, but in the 1860s the navy realised that iron-clad ships were much less easily damaged in battles at sea, and the building of wooden ships declined rapidly.

Another industry, the tanning of leather, was also expanding, and created a great demand for the bark of oak trees. Oak bark became a very valuable woodland product, as it was the best source of tannin, the substance used in the most common method of tanning leather. The skins were soaked in pits containing the tanning liquor for several months, until the process was complete. The bark was worth about a third as much as the timber and wood when an oak tree was felled[10].

Landowners

We have now considered some of the main events and changes in the 18th and 19th centuries which either directly or indirectly affected the state of woodland in Britain, and the working conditions of those involved. Before going on to examine in detail the actual work being carried out in the coppices, the management of large country estates at that time needs to be considered. By and large woodland had been retained by landowners on ground which was either too steep to cultivate easily, or which was heavy, intractable clay, or very light poor soil. Woodland was an economic use for such land, as it provided wood for use on the estate, and mature timber trees as a long-term financial investment.

There was a growing realisation in Parliament during the late 17th and early 18th centuries that both woodland and hedgerow trees in this country had been decimated, and that steps to improve the situation were required. Legislation was therefore passed to try and encourage better management of woodland on both Crown and private land. An Act was passed in 1715 :

An Act to encourage the Planting of Timber-Trees, Fruit-Trees, and other Trees, for Ornament, Shelter or Profit; and for better Preservation of the same; and for Preventing the Burning of Woods

Parishes were made liable to owners for malicious damage to timber trees. The woodland deficit still existed fifty years later:

An Act for encouraging the Cultivation, and for the better Preservation of Trees, Roots, Plants and Shrubs

This Act in 1766 related to timber trees and was closely followed by another in the same year, which added a number of additional tree species to be encouraged. In 1793 there was a lengthy report on the condition of woodland on Crown land which expressed great concern about the loss of mature trees in the country as a whole[11].

There is much concern repeatedly expressed that timber is being felled excessively (particularly oak). Hedgerow oaks are particularly good specimens for the Navy.

There is not a doubt but that the country formerly was much more woody than at present, and the land has been converted to tillage, for on the one hand the Navy has greatly increased both in number and size, so has commerce likewise, which has occasioned great consumption of timber; so on the other, Population has also increased, which has required more land for cultivation into arable and pasture, for the support of the inhabitants and cattle.

The result was the Timber Preservation Act of 1808, as an attempt to increase timber production in Crown forests.

The condition of the woodland was such that large-scale plantations were considered vital. In the early 18th century about 1000 acres in the New Forest were enclosed and planted with acorns[12]. As silviculture improved, young nursery-grown trees began to be used routinely for planting. William Cobbett in 1822 on his ride from Kensington to Uphusband (Hurstbourne Tarrant)[13] noted plantations of hazel and ash near Andover, and applauded the planters for having trenched the ground and planted small trees. He was less enthusiastic about their attempts to bring up the sub-soil to the surface.

During the 18th century it became fashionable for wealthy landowners to landscape the area around their country houses with parks and woodland. In addition to plantations of native trees, many exotic species were imported and planted, to become a magnificent spectacle a hundred years later, for the pleasure of their descendants. An outstanding example of grand design coupled with practical timber production is the woodland which was laid out in Savernake Forest by successive generations of the Bruce family. Long avenues of trees, radiating from a central point, divided up the oak plantations, and a broad ride led away from the house towards a stone column on the opposite hillside.

Bentley Wood was managed on a rather more modest scale but it is interesting to note that the Amesbury part of the wood belonged to the Bruce family, from 1676 until 1720, just before their landscaping of Savernake. During the 18th century Bentley Wood was still divided between five different owners, only one of whom lived in the immediate locality and hence they had no incentive to plant trees for purely aesthetic reasons or to landscape the wood as a whole. The wood did, however, form the backdrop to the view across the park from Norman Court (Fig.27), the elegant new mansion built by Robert Thistlethwaite in the 1750s. The present house, on its elevated site, replaced the original smaller one which stood near the West Dean road entrance to Norman Court farm.

Timber, particularly oak, represented a long-term investment to the landowner, but once the trees had reached a suitable size, it was a valuable commodity which could be sold easily for a good price. In spite of the need to build up timber supplies in the country, the introduction of inheritance tax was a disincentive to very long-term investment, though there were some concessions for standing timber[14]. A landowner had traditionally managed timber for future generations of his own family, and an inheritance tax discouraged replanting slow-growing trees.

Fox hunting was already a popular sport among country landowners and during the 19th century improvements in guns and ammunition increased the popularity of game shooting. Birds could be hit at a longer range and the guns could be re-loaded quickly, making shooting of game birds an attractive pastime for estate owners. Enthusiastic landowners made a considerable investment in their sport, and began to manage woodland with shooting pheasants in mind. The excessive zeal with which the landed gentry pursued their sporting interests made an ideal subject for the cartoonists of the day, such as John Leech with his drawings for Punch (Fig.28). Coppiced woodland was an ideal environment for such birds. Greater numbers of gamekeepers were taken on, who artificially reared large numbers of pheasants under domestic hens, before releasing them into the local woodland. The gamekeeper began to take precedence over the forester, sometimes to the detriment of the woodland[15]. Table 2 is an account of the game killed in the Amesbury part of Bentley Wood between 1757 and 1761 and it shows the relative numbers of the various species which had been shot[22]. Unfortunately no records of shooting in and around Bentley Wood during the 19th century have survived, but it is known that there were gamekeepers on the Norman Court estate.

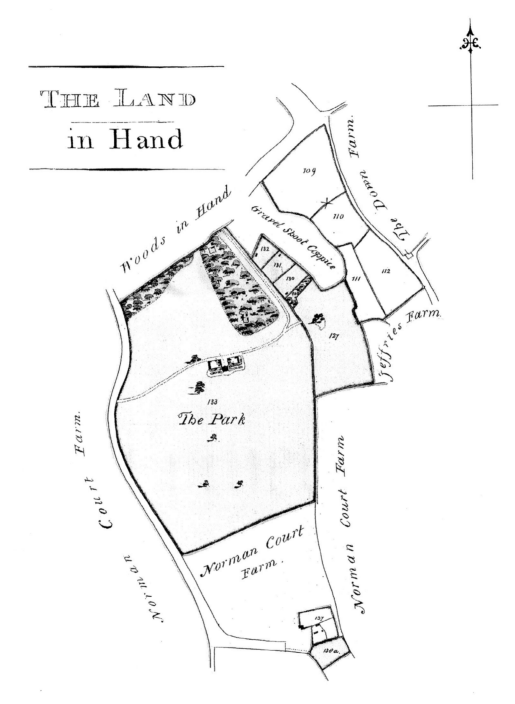

THE LAND in Hand

Fig 27 *Norman Court house and park from the 1807 estate survey.*
(HCRO ref 85M71PZ2)

Table 2.

"Account of game killed at Bently Woods by Richard Bloxham and delivered at His Graces the Duke of Queensberry's at Amesbury".

Year	Hares	Cock Pheasants	Partridge	Woodcocks
1757-58	41	22	46	8
1758-59	47	32	17	8
1759-60	52	36	27	12
1760-61	43	32	15	52

Woodland Management

Bentley Wood throughout this time remained deciduous woodland, managed in a traditional way as coppice-with-standards. A survey and valuation of the Amesbury estate part of the wood in 1813[16] gives a valuable insight into the condition of the coppices at that date. In the survey (See Appendix II) the standard trees are almost all oak, with very small numbers of ash, maple and beech. There is no information to indicate what species make up the underwood, but this would have been predominantly hazel, for which there was the greatest demand. There was likely to have been some coppiced ash, which also grows well on the chalk soil, and which would have been used locally for scythe and rake handles and other farm tools. The underwood may have been coppiced after variable time intervals, but the survey indicates that ten or eleven years was normally the longest cycle allowed. The large number of oak trees present in each coppice suggests that the timber had not been cut too heavily during the second half of the 18th century.

The 1874 Ordnance Survey map shows that almost the entire wood was deciduous standard trees and coppice. The only part of the wood shown to contain conifers is Richwellstead Copse, owned at that time by Roche Court, Winterslow, which appears to have been mixed woodland. In general, where woodland was cleared and completely replanted, the area usually became

SPORT(?) FOWL SHOOTING.

THE FEROCIOUS PHEASANTS THINK THEY ARE GOING TO BE FED, AND SURROUND THE HONOURABLE MR. BATTUE ACCORDINGLY.

A SHORT CUT THROUGH THE WOOD.

Fig 28 *Mid-19th century cartoons from Punch by John Leech.*

renamed as "plantation". All of the old names throughout Bentley Wood are as "coppice", which suggests that there was no great change from the traditional coppice management.

Cutting The Coppice

An invaluable account of how coppice work was carried out locally is to be found in the books of Michael Parsons, "The Brittle Thread" and "Chips and Chumps", two of a series of monographs on the local history of Farley and Pitton. He writes with the authenticity of one who came from a family who earned their living by the sale of coppiced wood, and who had first-hand knowledge of woodland work in the 20th century. All of his books are available in Salisbury Reference Library.

Areas of standing coppice were traditionally sold when the stools had about ten years' growth on them. Annual auctions took place for the combined local estates, and local woodmen would buy a "lot" of underwood to be cut and removed by themselves and their families during the winter months. The different sections in a coppice were bounded by cart-tracks a certain distance

Fig 29 *Coppice work. (R Pearce)*

apart. Linear measurement was in woodland luggs or rods (6yds) and area in woodland acres (5760 sq. yds.)

The cutting season began on November 1st, Old Martinmas, when entry into the coppices was permitted and work could start. Some coppices were more desirable than others, but in the 19th century hazel, ash, beech, maple, birch and hornbeam were all considered highly usable species. The purchase of the underwood did not include timber trees, tellers or saplings, which remained the property of the landowner.

The wood was cut using hooks and hatchets; it was not cut with a saw. It was then sorted into different sizes for sale for different purposes. Much of the hazel was sold for making wattle hurdles and thatching spars, but there was also a thriving market for bean poles and pea sticks. The heaviest poles were cleft into lengths for gate hurdles and fence palings. Ash was used for the handles of scythes, brooms and rakes. An essential use of the wood was fuel, and bundles of wood were bound together for this purpose, known as bavins, and faggots. Bavins contained poles up to six feet in length and were used for heating bread ovens; faggots were small bundles of firewood.

One acre of good coppice could be cut and sorted by one man in a week, and might yield 25 dozen sheep hurdles, 200-300 bundles of pea sticks and 15 bundles of bean poles.

An interesting insight into coppice life in the 18th century is to be found in the working account book of another Parsons of Farley, John Parsons, which he kept in the 1780s (Fig.30). John was in charge of managing woodland on the Ilchester estate in Farley and Pitton, but he also seems to have been responsible for selling coppices in Bentley and other estates and his accounts are written in a notebook. He did not buy a new one, but wrote his name on the back cover of an old, half-used mathematics exercise book and started his accounts from that end of the book. The book, in a rather fragile condition, is still in the hands of a present-day descendant.

The book records sales of standing coppice in Bentley Wood, along with coppice in the Farley and Clarendon area (Appendix III). In 1782 he sold 160 luggs of standing wood in Hawksgrove in December. In the following February he sold another 80 luggs to Samuel Light and 21 luggs to Joseph Hatcher, both in Hawksgrove. In 1784 he sold 192 luggs in Coalpits Coppice First side to Mr. Bloxam and 168 luggs of Coalpits the left side to Mr. Brown. A "side" was an area of the wood. Mr. Bloxam bought up large areas of coppice in the Farley district, in 1784 he bought 529 luggs in Barnridge among his other purchases.

John Parsons also bought some of the standing wood himself, and in 1785 his accounts for the sale of the cut wood from Coalpits Copse show a typical coppice yield.

Mapleway, a corner of which was sold in 1782, was the only other part of Bentley Wood recorded in the book. "Corner" was another word used to denote a division of land.

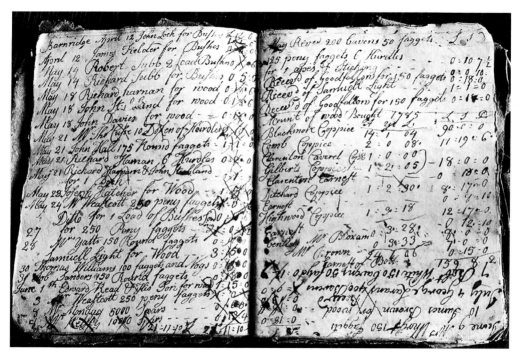

Fig 30 *John Parsons' book, 1767.(Chris Walker)*

Similar records for the sale of lots of standing underwood exist in the Duke of Queensberry's Amesbury estate timber accounts 1753-58[24]. Some cut timber was also sold, including 12 oak trees in Smokeway Copse, which fetched £12 (5 ton at £2 a ton and the tops valued at £2). The bark was sold for £1 5s.

Timber sales were another feature of estate and woodland management, but the cycle was naturally much longer than for the underwood. Considerable quantities of timber would have been used on the estate itself, but the surplus provided a good income. Timber trees sold for much higher prices than the coppiced wood, but it was only an occasional harvest, whereas the hazel produced a crop every 5-10 years. Oaks were cut at about 70 years old, depending on what the timber was needed for. They were not usually left to become magnificent specimen mature trees, as that would not only have been uneconomic, but would have increased the work of felling and the subsequent carpentry needed to turn the tree trunks into beams and planks. In the days before mechanisation trees were chosen which were as near as possible to the size of the finished product. Oak commanded the highest price as it was strong and durable and was the most favoured wood for building construction. Its durability meant that it could also be used outdoors for fences and gates.

Other, cheaper, timbers also had a variety of uses. Beech is not very durable and was rarely used in exposed locations, but it is fairly strong and its flexibility made it suitable for shaping for furniture. It was used extensively for internal fittings and carved well. Ash is a tough timber with considerable elasticity, which made it popular for the rims of wheels, cart shafts and tool handles. Elm is another not very durable wood which was useful for internal fittings and traditionally was used for coffins. Its durability increases when immersed in water, which made it a useful wood for making the keel of boats. A less common, and more expensive, timber is yew. However, yew trees grow readily on the chalk soils around the Norman Court estate and the surrounding countryside and yew was therefore probably used locally. The traditional use of yew for making archery bows had long since passed by the 19th century but it was highly prized for making fine quality furniture and as a beautiful yew veneer. Such furniture was not to be seen in cottages, but it might have been displayed in the mansion house. Smaller pieces were apparently used around the estate and one old yew gate post was finally removed in 2004. It had rotted at the base but was otherwise still very sound.

A sale of oak trees from the Norman Court estate in 1890 to timber merchants in Horsham, Sussex included 414 oaks from various parts of Bentley Wood, which were sold at 1s 9d per foot[25]. The haulage from West Tytherley to Horsham must have been a considerable undertaking but was presumably made possible by the close proximity of the railway and the wood was probably dispatched from West Dean station. There are also records dated 1890-93 of sales of beech, ash, elm, fir and a few willow from the estate as a whole, all to Mr. East of Tytherley. There was some variation in price, presumably depending on the size and quality of the trees, but beech and fir were 1s per foot and elm was 10d[26].

Coppice Industries

Many country crafts accompanied the cutting of the coppice. Wattle hurdle making (Fig.37) was a thriving local trade around Winterslow and Farley, since Wiltshire was sheep country. Large flocks grazed the downland, both locally and right across Salisbury Plain. The old, traditional way of fertilising the arable fields was to drive the sheep down each night onto the land before it had been ploughed, and pen them with hurdles onto a small area overnight, so that the dung was dropped onto that piece of the field and well trodden in. The hurdles were moved daily, so that the whole field was fertilised evenly. This labour-intensive tradition was gradually discontinued as part of the changes and improvements in the management of agricultural land. Hurdles were still required, however, as turnips were introduced as winter food for the sheep which were penned to graze a small area at a time. Another use of hurdles was to make small pens for individual sheep, either at lambing time, or in markets and sales. The wattle hurdles did not have a very long life, and the large numbers of sheep kept in Wiltshire ensured that the woodland areas in the southern part of the county always had a good market for their products. Gate hurdles were also used for making sheep pens, and when Salisbury market place was the site of the Tuesday livestock market, local hurdles were in regular demand.

Hurdle making always took place in the coppices, but other tasks, such as the making of thatching spars (Fig.38) could be carried out in a shed under cover. Spars are wooden pegs made of hazel which were traditionally used to secure the uppermost layer when constructing a thatched roof. Very large numbers were used locally as a high proportion of cottage roofs were thatched, and the tradition is still carried on today when the few remaining thatched roofs are repaired. Sheep cribs and farm implements were some of the other products made from the coppiced wood. When oak trees were felled such products as fence palings and wooden roof shingles were made. In the 20th century Norman Court had a paling fence, made locally, which encircled most of the estate.

Another important activity which had to be undertaken when oak trees were felled was barking. Immediately after felling the trees were sawn up into suitable lengths and the smaller branches removed. The bark was pulled off in strips with a rining tool and stacked to dry for a week or two. It was then transported to the tanneries at Downton or Romsey where it was used for tanning leather.

Fig 31 *Woodland crafts – making thatching spars. (R Pearce)*

Local woodland labourers were traditionally allowed some wood for their own use as fuel. Until the end of the 19th century they could take home whatever they could carry under one arm at the end of the day. Fuel was of vital importance to village families, and a regular supply of free wood helped their breadline economy considerably. William Cobbett commented in one of his Rural Rides (to Battle in 1822)[13] that woodland and forest workers were more fortunate than other rural labourers, whose lot in the 19th century was indeed a wretched one. In his words:

The coppices give them pleasant and profitable work in winter ... And then in the great article of fuel! They buy none. It is miserable work where this is to be bought, and where, as at Salisbury, the poor take by turns the making of fires at their houses to boil four or five tea kettles. What a winter-life must those lead whose turn it is not to make the fire!

Poachers

Poaching was a rural tradition which began when the Norman kings prohibited the capture or killing of certain species of wild animals by anyone who did not have specific permission to do so. Before that time anyone could hunt wild animals, as man had always done since prehistoric times. Under the Normans preservation of game, particularly deer, was not just for sport; venison was an important part of the king's wealth. In later times, particularly in the 18 and 19th centuries, estate owners protected the game species on their land purely for sport, and reared pheasants under hens to increase the numbers. Not surprisingly, they regarded these birds as their own property after release.

Country people always retained the feeling that it was their right to hunt wild animals, a right which had been usurped, initially by the king, and later by the landowning gentry. Consequently poaching was not regarded by the villagers as a serious criminal offence. In the days when feeding the family was a struggle, adding a rabbit to the stew-pot meant a good meal for once. It was also a sport, and as such persisted long after the need to capture wild animals to eke out a subsistence diet. In the 19th century the poaching of rabbits, hares and pheasants became a major cottage industry in the local villages[17,18].

Since venison was valuable, deer poaching in areas where deer were plentiful became an organised and often violent crime. Legislation was therefore introduced from time to time which increased the penalties for those caught in the act. In 1722 the so-called Black Act was passed to deal with deer stealing which included transportation for a second offence. Later in the 18th century penalties were increased for poaching at night.

Bentley Wood, from Norman times onwards, had its share of poachers. The earliest known reported incident was a case presented to the forest eyre of 1256[19], when a red deer, shot with two arrows, was found in Bentley Wood on St. Valentine's day, together with a mastiff from a house in Winterslow. In 1718 Humphry Bloxham, the estate gamekeeper in Bentley, was authorised by Lord Bruce, owner of Amesbury Manor, to:

take and seize according to Law all greyhounds, setting dogs, lurchers, Gunns, netts and all other Ingines and Instruments whatsoever made or made use of for Destruction of Game[23]

More recently, Henry East of West Tytherley was convicted in 1821 of being in Bentley Wood at night, and sentenced to 7 years transportation[18]. In the same year Henry Morgan, a shepherd, was fined £5, or a jail sentence if he could not pay, when convicted of wiring a hare near Buckholt on land belonging to Baring Wall[18]. Such sentences sound excessive in the 21st century, but they were similar to what was considered just punishment for other crimes in the 1820s.

Although a few local poachers were caught and subsequently punished by the courts, most poaching exploits have passed unrecorded except in family tradition and village folklore. Michael Parsons[18] and Ralph Whitlock[17] give good descriptions of poachers from the local parishes, both detected and undetected, in Victorian times. Throughout the 20th century most country people drew the distinction between organised deer stealing for the blackmarket venison trade, and small-time poaching, and condoned, or applauded, the thrills and skills involved in the latter. The demise of opportunistic minor poaching as a village tradition is mainly due to the loss of that expertise, beautifully described 50 years ago in Ian Niall's The Poacher's Handbook[20], in today's rural population.

Fig 32 *Poachers. (R Pearce)*

7

Coppice Names

An interesting feature of Bentley Wood for those who visit it frequently is the old coppice names, many of which have been used since the early 18th century, and some of them for very much longer. The names below are those used on maps based on the 1874 Ordnance Survey (Fig.33). Almost all the areas are called "coppice", indicating that they were, or had been, coppiced woodland.

In addition to the Ordnance Survey maps, the names of coppices can be found on the 18th and 19th century estate maps. A useful source for the origin of some of them is the Place Names of Wiltshire[1]. Unfortunately, in many cases it only gives the first recorded date for the names, rather than the derivation, which was presumably not known.

The structure and management of the wood changed little for many centuries before 1874, and some of the names used to distinguish different parts of the wood may have been in existence for a long time. However, literacy among rural labourers is relatively recent and few would have been able to write before the mid 19th century. The names, used daily in the wood by the people working there, would have been perpetuated by the oral tradition, in a strong Wiltshire accent or dialect. It is not therefore surprising that words sometimes changed, and were corrupted into something with a different meaning.

In 1885 the Rev. GS Master, rector of West Dean, wrote a list of local names, including many coppice names from Bentley Wood, and gave what he thought might have been the derivation[2]. The list below is our attempt, but we make no claim that it is any more accurate.

Wood. From *wudu* Old English (OE).

Bentley. From *beonet* and *leah* (OE) meaning the clearing where bent grass grows. Written in various ways, such as Bentelwoda, and first recorded in the 13th century[1].

Clarendon. From *caefren-dun* (OE) meaning clover-grown hill[1].

Fig 33 *Coppice boundaries and names taken from information on the 1874 OS map.*
(M Baskerville)

Dean. From *denu* meaning valley. Recorded as Duene in the Domesday Book.

Richwellstead Copse. Given on the edge of the Amesbury Estate map[3] of 1726 as Headons Coppice. Recorded on the Winterslow tithe map in 1837 as Richwellstead. "Wellsteads Piece" on the same map was an area adjacent to Norman Court North Lodge, which suggests that the occupier of both had been a man called Richard Wellstead. He was not the current occupier.

Coppices were sometimes named because of their shape.

Picked Copse. First recorded in 1540 as Pykkyd Copse[14]. Picked means pointed or tapering.

Redman's Gore. First recorded in 1726[3] as Redman Gore. A gore is a triangular piece of ground (English Place-Names)[4]. Redman was a local surname.

Some coppice names describe the trees which must have been a feature at some time.

Beechways Copse. First recorded in 1540[14] as Beche ways. One or more of the tracks were probably lined with beeches.

Beechwood Copse. First recorded as Beechwood Coppice on the West Dean tithe map in 1843.

Elm's Copse. First recorded on the 1874 OS map. The apostrophe is probably a mistake on the map. The name had recently changed from Bushy Common.

Mapleway Dean Copse. First recorded in 1540[14] as Maple Dene. See above for origin of Dean.

High Bushes. First recorded in 1843 as High Bushes Coppice on the West Dean tithe map.

Most of the names describe the coppice in some way.

Churchway Copse. First recorded circa 1800 on the map of Dean Wood[5] as Churchway Coppice. The route from East Grimstead to the parish church at West Dean ran along the southern boundary.

Coalpits Copse. First recorded in 1540[14] as Collpytts Copse. It is likely to have been the site of early charcoal burning. It could have originated as far back as Saxon times, since *col pyttes* is the Old English word. Charcoal production in an earth-covered kiln had replaced the use of pits by the 16th century but the woodland kiln site was still referred to as a "pitstead".

Smokeways Copse. First recorded in 1540[14] as Smokkways. This also was probably another charcoal burning site. However, a possible derivation is from Smoke-money, or Smoke-penny, which was a levy payable to the church when coppice was cut down[6].

Highwood Copse. First recorded in 1279[1]. Highwood is a corruption of Haywood from (*ge*)haeg (OE) meaning enclosure.

Hawksgrove. First recorded in 1843 as Hawksgrove Coppice on the West Dean tithe map. Grove is derived from graf (OE) meaning thicket or small wood[7].

Park Copse. First recorded in the 1807 survey of Norman Court estate. It was not a single copse, but was divided into small areas with different names.

Prior's Copse. A 14th century perambulation of Clarendon Forest refers to "Preyerswode", the modern Prior's Copse[8]. The nuns in Amesbury Priory were entitled to a daily cartload of wood from Bentley Wood at that time, and this would seem to be the most likely connection. To confuse the issue, a Sir Harry Preyers held the manor of West Tytherley in the 14th century, but this seems a less likely origin.

Cowley's Copse. First recorded in 1843 as Cowlease on the West Dean tithe map. It lies adjacent to what was the field "Cowlease" on the 1807 Survey of Norman Court Estate. Sometime between 1843 and the 1874 OS map it had become corrupted to Cowley's.

Hatchers Copse. First recorded as Hatcher's Coppice on the map of Dean Wood circa 1800[5]. The most likely derivation is from haecce (OE), or hatch, meaning gate. The copse lay on the edge of the wood where there could have been a gate into the adjacent field. Another possible origin is from Archer, a common local name, frequently corrupted to Hatcher. However, this is less likely as the land belonging to the Archers was not in this immediate area.

Barnridge. First recorded in 1365 as Bardenrigge[1]. Ridge or rigg is from hrycg (OE) meaning ridge. Recorded as Barne Rydge in 1540[14].

Redridge. First recorded in 1540[14] as Reddrydge Copse. Red is possibly from reed, *hreod* (OE) or from the soil colour.

Howe Copse. First recorded in 1800 on the Dean Wood map[5] as How Coppice. It was land originally belonging to Howe Farm, which was first recorded as la Howe in 1362. Howe is derived from *hoh, hoe* (OE) meaning hill or hill spur[1].

Heath Copse and Dean Heath. The south eastern end of Bentley Wood was open common land in the 16-17th centuries1[4,9]. Dean Heath later became Beechwood Copse and Bushey Common became Elm's Copse. Heath Copse was coppice by 1800[5] and was listed as woodland on the West Dean tithe apportionment in 1843.

Donkey Copse. First recorded in 1820 on an estate map of West Dean[10] as Asses Coppice. Presumably there had been a resident donkey, or donkeys, grazing there, which suggests wood pasture. It was not very new coppice in 1820, as it was cut in 1827[10].

New Berryfield. There were 3 fields and a coppice called Berryfield in West Dean in the 19th century. Berry and Bury are common elements in field names, usually denoting that they lie near the manor, or an earthwork[1], and there are both in West Dean village. It was called New Coppice in 1820[10]. However, berrie, or burie, can signify a former rabbit warren[11].

Dean Copse. On the 1820 estate map of West Dean, Dean Copse is not shown as a single coppice, but as a row of small unnamed ones. These are all called "Berryfield" on the tithe map in 1843.

Beegarden Copse. This appears as Fair Grove Coppice in 1800 on the Dean Wood map[5], and again on the West Dean tithe map. It is first recorded as "Beegarden Copse" on the 1874 OS map. Bee gardens were small enclosed areas in which bee skeps were placed so that farm animals could not interfere with them.

Three Sisters Copse. First recorded in 1540[14] as 3 Systers. It is tempting to look for three sisters somewhere in the history of the wood. An obvious choice would be the three Waleran sisters who were given the southern part of Bentley Wood by Ela, Countess of Salisbury in 1227. Ela also owned the Northern end of the wood, including Three Sisters Copse. However, woodland coppice names were invariably simple descriptive words used by the village people to distinguish one part of the wood from another. To name a coppice in the middle of a wood after three society ladies would be unlikely.

A more plausible alternative would be a tree, or a group of trees. Notable trees were often used as boundary markers in woodland to define an area. A survey of Clarendon Park in 1650 lists Fair Oak, Kytes Ash and Cross Oak on woodland boundaries; more significantly there was also an "oake tree called the two sisters"[12]. Grovely Wood has a Four Sisters Copse.

Hooping Oak Copse. First recorded in 1540[14] as Whoping Oke. This would probably have been a particularly notable oak tree, or one used as a boundary marker. Barrel hoops held the staves of an oak barrel, or cask, together. They were usually made of ash, but hazel, oak and chestnut were also used. The men who made them were known as hoopers.

Rowley and Rowley Marsh (now Barnridge Meadow). First recorded in 1540 as "a comen callyd Rowley grene"[14]. Rowley coppice is recorded on the Amesbury estate map[3]. GS Master[2] gives the derivation as a corruption of Rough Leigh. Rowley Marsh (Fig.20) is the area between Barnridge and Coalpits coppices shown on the map of Dean Wood[5].

Armitage Copse. First recorded in 1540[14] as Armytage Copse. The name is derived from Hermitage[4] and it was recorded as Hermitage Copse on the West Dean tithe map. The name did not appear on the 1874 or subsequent OS maps. Hermits were common in Anglo-Saxon and medieval forests, where they lived a solitary, spiritual existence. They were often provided for by the local population. Hermits were the fore-runners of monastic communities. Unfortunately, nothing is known about our hermit.

Cook's Common. First recorded in 1800 on the map of Dean Wood[5]. Cook's tenement, or dwelling, is recorded on the "ffarelye mappe" of 1665 (WCRO) along Livery Road, Farley, near Blackmoor Copse. The map also shows a long stretch of common land, from Farley to Bentley Wood. Cook's Common joined onto the end of this, and is part of Farley parish.

Pegsbrook Copse. First recorded in 1348[1] as Peykesbrouk. It is likely to have been a "picked" or pointed copse with a brook[13].

Pheru. First recorded in 1540[14] as Fayre yewe. Presumably a large yew tree grew within, or on the bounds of, the coppice.

Other names in the wood.

Marigold Beech. This was shown on some early 20th century maps. It was a notable beech tree which was a familiar boundary mark until World War II[13].

Pound Ride. (Fig. 48) The name probably originated from the banked enclosure next to the track. When domestic animals were regularly foraging around the wood there would have been a pound or stockade where stray or illegal animals were impounded. Villagers were restricted in the number of animals that they could graze on an area of common land, and they had to pay a fine to recover any illegal ones which had been rounded up into the pound.

Although it may have been used as a pound, the banked enclosure could well be the remains of a prehistoric farmstead.

Blackmore/Blackmoor Hill. First recorded in 1540 as Black mare hyll[14]. It is shown on the map of Dean Wood (Fig.12) between Barnridge and what is now Blackmoor Copse. It was part of the Howe Farm area of Bentley. Blackmore was the marshy land stretching from the hill towards Farley. The word "more" was originally used to denote a low-lying wet area rather than high heathland. Blackmore Hill appears to have been rough grazing land or "comen", there are no descriptions of it as coppice.

Mary Grave. Recorded on the edge of the Amesbury estate map at the point where the bridle path across the wood meets Park Lane (Livery Track)[3]. This is probably the 12 acres of common called "Mery Grove corn(er) in 1540[14]. It may have been a pleasant, or 'myrig' place[1]; alternatively "mere" can mean a boundary, which would be appropriate in this case. In 1807 it was called Parkway coppice.

8

Pits

A striking feature of Bentley Wood is the pits; the woodland floor is pockmarked with hollows of all shapes and sizes. The majority are in the northern part of the wood but there are some dotted around throughout. A few of the pits are very large, both wide and deep, with the remains of a track into the pit still visible, but by far the most numerous are the cup-shaped, steep-sided depressions. These vary considerably in size, but are typically about 20 metres in diameter and 2 metres deep. There are also many small irregular depressions. With one or two exceptions all of the pits are dry in the base, except in very wet weather. Most have trees growing in them, and some have old coppice stools growing out of the walls which have obviously been there for a long time.

An examination of the countryside outside the wood quickly reveals that pits are not unique to Bentley Wood. There are numerous similar pits everywhere; in fields, in woodland and by the roadside. They are often very overgrown and many roadside pits can easily be missed unless one is looking out for them. Pits in ground which holds water appear as ponds and unfortunately it is hard to see the original size and shape of a pond if it is permanently filled with water.

Early large-scale OS maps of the countryside around Bentley Wood show numerous pits, particularly in fields, often marked "pit disused" or "old chalk pit". They were an old feature even in the late 19th century. OS maps show very big pits only, smaller ones are not recorded.

Other parts of the country also have their share of pits. The New Forest, for example, has 329 ponds, many of which are water-filled artificial pits, where marl or clay have been extracted. Some are bomb craters[1]. Dyer[7] comments that

disused marl pits remain one of the enduring legacies of pre-industrial agriculture – seventy have been recorded in one Worcester parish

Rackham in his "History of the Countryside"[2] devotes a whole chapter to Ponds, Dells and Pits. He defines a pit as an artificial depression in the ground, without water; if it is apparently natural it is termed a dell. Ponds are water-filled depressions, either natural or artificial.

Hollows and depressions in the ground may be due to natural causes, as for example the small hollow made when a tree blows over, upending the root plate. A geological cause sometimes encountered in chalk and limestone areas is a swallow hole, of which there are examples in Pegsbrook and Lower Highwood Copses in Bentley Wood[3]. Chalk dissolves in rainwater, particularly in acid conditions associated with rotting vegetation, and drains away downwards, forming a track through the underlying chalk. A surface hollow is formed, and if water runs into it, it disappears, following the same track. However, such natural features cannot explain all the hollows in the wood.

Artificial depressions are due to human activity, particularly mineral extraction, which has been taking place since man first colonised Britain. The nature and shape of such workings depends on what has been extracted, and the scale of the enterprise. The underlying geology of the ground can vary considerably over a short distance, and early man must have worked very hard exploring the earth beneath his feet to locate the best deposits of the minerals he needed. In areas where there is no building stone near the surface, old workings and depressions are likely to have been for chalk, gravel or clay. In some areas underground extraction, for coal, salt or flint may cause the ground above to collapse, thereby causing a surface depression. There is no evidence of underground extraction in Bentley Wood.

In regions such as the south of Wiltshire where there is chalk subsoil, extracting it accounts for many of the pits to be found in the countryside. Chalk has been used as a building material, and for making firm floor surfaces for dwellings and barns since Roman times. Excavation of the East Grimstead Roman villa revealed that the walls were of chalk rubble construction, and the floors were made of puddled chalk[4]. During the following 2000 years, until the 20th century, chalk was being used for similar purposes in the local villages. Chalk rubble is still sometimes used today to make very serviceable firm tracks and as a floor for barns and stables.

By far the greatest volume of chalk has been used on the land to improve the yield of agricultural crops. This has already been discussed in chapter 6, as much of it was used as part of the agricultural improvements of the 18th and 19th centuries. Natural chalk, either rough or crushed, was still being taken from small farm chalk pits to be spread on the land in thc mid 20th century.

Another much-used mineral found in chalk areas is flint. Flints, particularly broken fragments, can be found scattered all over arable fields where the subsoil is chalk, but better specimens were often taken directly from the underlying chalk. Flints could therefore either be a by-product from a chalk pit or quarry, or a pit could be sunk in the ground where the flints were thought to be particularly good ones. The use of flint as a building material has been common practice in the villages and farms around Bentley Wood since Roman times. Not only were whole or part flints incorporated in the substance of walls, but knapped flints were used to make an extremely durable and attractive exterior surface, which can still be seen on local churches and country houses.

Large chalk pits are easily recognised. Even when they are very overgrown, removal of the soil and surface debris soon reveals the underlying chalk. Any rabbit burrows or badger setts usually have a heap of chalk at the entrance. A track down into the pit can often be seen, though chalk pits on hilltops which have been sunk down through the clay cap may have very steep sides all round. Most of the very large man-made pits in Bentley Wood, such as the one just south of the Livery Track and the pit in Churchways, are readily identifiable as chalk pits. A similar, though slightly smaller, chalk pit in which there is an identifiable track leading into the pit can be seen in Three Sisters Copse.

In Bentley Wood far more numerous are the smaller bowl-shaped pits (Fig.24), and many, or most, of these are likely to be marl (chalky clay), chalk or flint pits also. A closer look at the distribution of them shows that most of them are in the northern part of the wood where the subsoil is chalk and many are close to access tracks. Significantly they are all dry pits, since any water collecting in them percolates rapidly down through the chalk below. To explain them one needs to consider the habits of village communities in the past. When they needed chalk, flints or gravel, they went out and dug a pit in the nearest convenient place. Pits were often dug on common land, but unauthorised digging was not allowed under the medieval manorial system[2]. By the 19th century, large village chalk pits were controlled by the parish overseer[5]. Where chalk and flints were readily available, they were convenient material for making up road and track surfaces, and when one considers the many miles of local lanes and tracks which needed repairing from time to time, it becomes easier to understand the purpose of the many chalk pits.

Uncultivated land, or woodland, provided that there was access, would have been a suitable place for digging chalk for building material, road repairs or for spreading on the fields. Ellis in 1772[6] comments:

But where a wood or spring adjoins to the field, or near it, then this situation may be most proper for sinking a pit.

The trees must have posed a problem for digging in a wood, and it is possible that seemingly rather inaccessible pits in Bentley Wood were dug there because it was an area clear of trees at the time. Subsequently trees grew up out of the pit walls, as Ellis[6] noticed:

Trees or other wood will nevertheless get up in a little time, spontaneously from the fibres of the adjacent roots, and then grow faster than ordinary in this hollow cavity of ground.

We do not know why there is such a large number of chalk pits in Bentley Wood. One reason could be that pits in woodland did not get filled in again, whereas those in the fields did. Ellis[6] comments on this:

By being in the center of the field, the plough, by traversing the ground on all sides, in time will bring down and drive the adjacent earth into it.

Evidence from old maps and aerial photographs supports this, as they show the remains of many more pits in the landscape surrounding the wood than are visible on the ground today.

There may also have been a local agreement that chalk and flints could be removed from the wood by the villagers. There is no local building stone and many cottages in the surrounding area over the last several hundred years have been built of chalk.

While chalk was the most frequently used material, some pits in the southern part of Bentley Wood may have been used for extracting other minerals. Clay was used for making bricks and tiles from Roman times onwards, and one would expect to find clay pits in places where the subsoil is clay. The West Dean Brickworks (see Chapter 9) was sited on the edge of Bentley Wood, where there was suitable clay for making bricks and tiles, to minimise transport of the raw material. There may be other, very old, clay pits around the southern part of the wood as well.

Sawpits leave small narrow grave-shaped pits. No obvious sawpits have been located in Bentley Wood, but such an origin should be considered if the collapsed remains of a small grave-shaped pit is found.

Another activity which produced small pits was charcoal production. The use of pits had been replaced by covered heaps on the surface by the 16th century, so it is not surprising that the remains of them are hard to find. However, they probably existed in Coalpits Copse. Any blackened ground, well below the present soil surface, in either Coalpits or Smokeways should be considered as a possible former charcoal pit.

Craters caused by bombs during World War II are another possible cause of artificial pits, and these are discussed in Chapter 10. A typical bomb crater is a conical hole surrounded by a bank of displaced earth[2]. The age of any trees or coppice stools growing within the pit may give a clue as to whether the pit was likely to have been formed more than 60 years ago. It is also possible that some of the existing chalk pits were enlarged during the occupation of the wood by troops in the last war, but after 60 years there are no obvious signs. Certainly they used at least one pit as a dump for all kinds of equipment before they left.

When looking at an individual pit it is not always possible to state categorically how, why or when, it was formed. The first impression can sometimes be deceptive, for natural slumping of the sides, or the tipping of soil and rubble into the pit, may have changed its shape. However, a closer look at the pit and the soil type in the area around, may give some indication of its origin.

9

The Singer Era

The end of the Victorian era and the dawn of the 20th century made little difference to rural workers in the coppices of Bentley Wood. The big changes in the story of the wood were changes of ownership. Francis Baring was the owner of Norman Court in the early 20th century, having inherited it from his father, William, who in turn had inherited from Thomas Baring. The estate was subsequently sold by Francis in 1906.

It was purchased by an American, Washington Singer, who recognized its great potential for establishing a race-horse stud by expansion of the existing stabling and areas for gallops. He was one of the sons of the American sewing-machine magnate, Isaac Singer. Washington had a great interest in horses and kept both hunters and racehorses. His interest expanded to include breeding and he had already built up a stud farm in Paignton, his family home before moving to West Tytherley. He put considerable effort into establishing the stud at Norman court, and the fields adjacent to Bentley Wood, particularly Golden Park on the eastern side, were used as gallops for training the horses.

The estate was well managed during Singer's time, and he paid considerable attention to his woodland as well as to his sporting interests. He did not, however, have any great financial need to maximize the timber production on the estate, and could allow such considerations as providing cover for his pheasants to be given due priority. He was regarded by most of his tenants living on the estate at Norman Court as a considerate and kindly landlord who financed the building of the village halls in West Tytherley and West Dean and provided jobs for most of the local population.

The Norman Court estate was expanded considerably during the years which followed its purchase in 1906. It included about 9000 acres at that time but when sold in 1945-46 the estate totalled 20,000 acres. Bentley Wood increased slightly in size, in 1920 Richwellstead Copse was purchased from Roche Court estate, and as a result the whole of the wood as we know it today came under a single ownership for the first time.

Fig 34 *Norman Court house as shown in the 1946 sale brochure.*
(HCRO ref 85M71PZ4)

Forestry policy in the early part of the 20th century

By the end of the 19th century wood had been largely superseded by coal as the major energy source in Britain. The increased demand for fuel created by the Industrial Revolution was met by coal mining, and the newly-available railway network allowed easy transport to all parts of the country. There was also a steep decline in the use of wood for ship building, as the vessels built for both the Navy and for merchant shipping were now made of steel. Large quantities of timber were still needed as pit-props in coal mines and for construction of factories and houses, as the population increased. However, much of the timber used in the industrial areas of Britain was being imported relatively cheaply from abroad in the early 1900s and consequently the country was unprepared for the sudden demand for home-grown timber in 1914 at the outbreak of war.

The turn of the century was the beginning of the end of the old era of forestry, which throughout southern England had been largely coppice or coppice-with-standards; the new era saw the rise of forestry as a science, with new developments in silviculture and plantation management to maximize the yield.

In 1902 a committee of the Board of Agriculture recommended that lecturers in forestry should be appointed at Oxford and Cambridge universities and that there should be courses for young foresters at agricultural colleges. An inquiry needed to be held on the area and composition of British woodland and local authorities were to be encouraged to plant trees in water catchment areas.

By 1910 there was a new appreciation of the technical aspects of forestry, particularly forest management and silviculture, and forestry courses had been instituted. However, the inadequacy of the country's woodland remained an increasing cause for concern and by 1914 many committees had sat to consider the problem, but had achieved very little. At the outbreak of World War I Britain was importing 400 million cubic feet of timber per year. There were reasonable stocks of imported wood in the country in 1914 and it was considered that the war would not create a heavy demand, but when merchant shipping began to suffer heavy losses rapid action had to be taken. British wood was then used as far as possible, and new sawmills had to be established to cope with the extra load. The war had highlighted the fact that timber, like coal and iron, was essential for the economy of the country.

During, and immediately after, the war at least 450,000 acres of woodland in Britain were felled. Softwoods (pine, spruce, fir) were needed in industry and coal mining, although hardwoods such as oak were still being used for some purposes. At this period Bentley Wood's mature tree species consisted mainly of hardwoods such as oak, ash and beech, with smaller amounts of softwoods (mainly Norway spruce and Scots pine). As a result, the wood did not suffer too much from cutting, although most of the oldest and largest oaks growing at the time in Dean Copse in the southern part of the wood were felled. The felled tree trunks were hauled up the 12 o'clock Ride on wheeled platforms running on lines, the trucks being pulled by horses. These oaks were about 120 years old at the time of World War I, having been planted in the late 18th and early 19th centuries. When the state of the country's woodlands and future timber supplies were looked at in the aftermath of World War I it was realised that the yield from the existing woodland was only about a third of what it could be under efficient management, and that the country had been relying heavily on imports. It was estimated that 2 million acres of the country's rough grazing land could be removed without a significant drop in meat production and put to better use by afforestation. This would have the added benefit of employing ten times the

Fig 35 *Steam power – a modern demonstration. (A Baskerville)*

number of men who had previously worked in the region. Rising unemployment was another problem which was causing concern at that time.

In 1919 the Forestry Commission was established to further the interests of forestry by promoting afforestation and timber production. They were empowered to buy or lease land, to acquire standing timber and to make grants or loans for private afforestation or replanting. They also gave advice on planting or managing woodland.

However, against this background of change much of the woodland in southern Britain remained as broadleafed trees, particularly oak, with coppice underwood. When the demand for timber declined at the end of the 19th century, and managing coppice became less profitable than it had been, many landowners had turned their woodland over to pheasant shooting rather than trying to improve the timber production. Many country estates such as Norman

Court continued to be organised much as they had been in the past, with perhaps the addition of a few limited areas of plantation.

In the early 20th century Bentley Wood was still managed as coppice-with-standards and the routine in the woodlands of south Wiltshire was very much as in former times. Coppice management was less economic than it had been a generation earlier, although there was still a local demand for sheep hurdles, thatching spars and implement handles. Sales of the local underwood still took place in the Black Horse public house or in the village hall in West Tytherley.

There are no indications that Washington Singer felled many mature trees during his 28 year-long ownership of the wood. He quickly re-planted Dean Copse with broadleaf trees, mainly oak, shortly after World War I. The only other change to the face of the wood in the early part of the 20th century occurred in the area of Smokeways and Prior's Copse between the years 1911-24, where about 100 acres of woodland were clear-felled and used as woodland pasture afterwards, probably for Singer's horses. Aerial photographs taken many years later by the Royal Air Force revealed ancient field systems in this pasture area. The Singers also introduced one or two small larch plantations.

The Decline of Coppice Industries

For many centuries hurdle making had been an important industry in south Wiltshire. The main uses of wattle hurdles were for making pens to hold sheep, and for making folds, or small enclosures, on the arable fields so that the ground could be manured and trodden by having a large number of sheep held in a small area overnight. Gate hurdles were used extensively in fairs and markets. Hurdle making was therefore heavily dependent on the fortunes of sheep farming. The prosperity of Wiltshire had been built on its sheep flocks, but the late 19th and early 20th centuries saw a steady reduction in the numbers of sheep in the county. In 1869 there were 808,658 sheep, which had dropped to 491,363 by 1909 and the numbers continued to decline, so that in 1925 there were only 258,895[5]. Although wool production had been important, it was always subordinate to the fertilisation of arable land with sheep manure. During the 19th century there was a decline in corn production in Britain due to increased imports from abroad and at the same time artificial nitrogenous fertilisers were

Fig 36 *Local hurdlemaker Ern Read splitting hazel.(Vic Collins)*

introduced, making the practice of penning sheep to manure the land unnecessary. Inevitably, this resulted in a general reduction in the sheep population and a decreased requirement for hurdles. Towards the end of the 19th century the decline in sheep numbers was exacerbated by an increased public demand for young lamb, killed at less than 12 months old, instead of eating older animals which had been kept for 2-3 years. Imported lamb and mutton from New Zealand increasingly affected the home market and, finally, the regular income from dairy herds became increasingly attractive to farmers, who reduced their sheep flocks accordingly.

Nevertheless, although the vast Wiltshire sheep flocks had declined in numbers, they were still an important part of the farm economy and hurdles continued to be used for penning sheep into lambing coops and in markets until after the second World War. The 20th century also saw the introduction of barbed wire, sheep netting and the electric fence, which meant that sheep could easily be contained in part of a field if necessary, and wire fencing replaced the hurdle as a means of stopping up a gap in a hedge or broken gate. In the later part of the century metal hurdles replaced the wooden wattle or gate hurdles for most farm purposes and the use of wattle hurdles in village gardens had also declined.

Other traditional woodland crafts were also slowly being replaced by new methods and materials. By the middle of the 20th century leather was being treated with tannin from tropical trees or with chemical substitutes, rather than with the traditional oak tannin. The advent of motorised vehicles heralded the decline of wooden carts and carriages, and beautifully crafted wooden wheels were replaced by metal ones with pneumatic tyres. The demand for hazel or oak barrel hoops declined as metal rings gradually became the accepted way of holding a barrel together.

However, the art of hurdle making has not completely died out, and in the 21st century has had a revival, albeit as a minor country craft, for garden hurdles and deer fencing. Thatching spars are also still being produced, for although there are very few new thatched roofs, the existing ones need regular replacement and maintenance.

A few new markets for the products of coppiced woodland opened up as the traditional ones declined. Michael Parsons describes some of the new outlets for

Fig 37 *Local hurdlemaker Fred Collins at work.(Vic Collins)*

local underwood in the Clarendon and Bentley area which his family exploited between the wars[1]. One of these was the production of fascines, or bundles of brush and thin copse poles, which were used for road and dock construction on soft or marshy ground. The fascines formed a good support for heavy foundations and lasted indefinitely in wet conditions. The idea was not a new one, similar bundles were placed under the foundations of both Winchester and Salisbury cathedrals. The bundles in Winchester were eventually replaced a thousand years later, in the early 20th century. During the 1930s large numbers of fascines were supplied by the Parsons family firm for the construction of a new dock in Southampton. Cutting and preparing them provided much-needed local employment during the Depression. In addition, they made large bundles of coppice poles to act as fenders to prevent damage to ships against dock walls.

Hazel rods were also sold for making crates for transporting crockery. Rods, 2-3 inches in diameter, were bent to form semi-rigid containers. The springy nature of the crates absorbed any shocks. A commercial use was found for birch in the production of vinegar and large quantities were made up into bundles and sent to Birmingham. The birch bark apparently encouraged the action of the vinegar fungus, *Mycodermum aceti*.

Many wooden products, such as tool handles, brush backs, besom brushes and ladders continued to be used and the wood to produce them was still in demand.

The dwindling market for coppice products in the late 19th and early 20th centuries also coincided with the decline in the use of wood as fuel. Although wood continued to be used in country districts where there was a ready supply, coal gradually replaced wood for both domestic and commercial heating.

The equipment and methods used in the coppices were still very much as they had been in the past. Significant mechanisation came later, after World War II, and until then hand saws, axes and bill hooks continued to be the tools of the trade.

Truffle Hunting

The old countryside traditions also continued into the 20th century. A local woodland industry which was still thriving in the early part of the century, particularly in Winterslow, was truffle hunting. Truffles are the underground tuber-like fruiting bodies of a fungus, and are principally found in woodlands on chalk or limestone. The most sought-after was *Tuber aestivum*, the black English truffle, but other varieties were also present and harvested. *T. aestivum* has a rough black surface and varies in size from very small up to walnut or even orange-sized, and it grows about a metre below the ground surface. The truffles were found most frequently in old beech woodland with hazel coppice[2].

In the mid-19th century truffle hunting provided seasonal work for 10-12 families in Winterslow, the season lasting from October or November through to March. The knowledge and expertise were maintained among certain local families, such as the Collins, Yates, Brays and Judds, and the tradition went back a long way in history. Fresh truffles have a powerful aroma which is made use of to locate them. In England dogs were trained to indicate where they were, but it also needed dog handlers with a wealth of experience of both truffle hunting and the local woodlands to find the right places. This knowledge was handed down the generations. The harvest could be very irregular and the number of truffles found sometimes varied considerably, even between villages in the same locality. In France the Perigord truffle, *T. melanosporum*, which is almost indistinguishable from *T. aestivum,* is still harvested today in orchards of walnut trees, using pigs instead of dogs to find them.

Truffles were a much-prized gastronomic delight to those who could afford them, and their scarcity always ensured that they commanded a high price, as it does today. An expert truffle hunter was therefore something of a celebrity in the past, and the hunters often worked the woodlands on estates over a wide area. Probably the best known local celebrity was Eli Collins of Winterslow, who had a special uniform provided for him by the Earl of Radnor, of Longford Castle, Salisbury[3].

The Forester

The general management of a big estate was carried out by the land agent, under the direction of the landowner. The agent often lived on the estate and he organised the daily routine work of the forester, including planting, felling and selling the timber. He was usually also responsible for farm tenancies and the

Fig 38 *Ern Read making thatching spars.(Vic Collins)*

upkeep of buildings on the estate. The Knapman family were the agents for Norman Court for many years and for much of the time an agent had lived in the Home Farm.

Under his direction, the forester was usually a local villager who, having started as a boy apprentice on the estate, had gradually risen through the ranks to reach the position. In the late 1930s the Norman Court estate forester was Mr.F.Christopher, of West Tytherley. He was responsible for overseeing all the woodland tasks, including the fencing, draining, planting, weeding, protection, felling and coppicing. Although the coppice was cut by independent workers, the forester made sure that they carried out the work competently. Saws were not allowed, and anyone found using a saw to cut the hazel instead of a bill-hook was removed from the wood. Workers were also dismissed if they were found building fires in Bentley Wood during the bird-nesting season. This rule was used to protect all ground-nesting birds, not only pheasant and woodcock. In those days pheasants were encouraged to nest in the wood to provide sport and food for the estate kitchens, unlike today, when thousands of imported poults are reared in pens before being released into the countryside. On the Singers' shoots the beaters, most of them estate workers, were allowed to take home a brace of birds if it had been a good day. Large estates such as Norman Court usually had several gamekeepers who organized shoots, serviced the guns, and kept a look-out for poachers.

Poaching continued to be a local pursuit and pastime, much as it had been in the 19th century. The coppice workers had ample opportunity to notice the whereabouts of hares and pheasants in the undergrowth as they went about their daily work, and a good supper was often the reward.

The Brickworks

Large country estates were still very self-contained in the first half of the 20th century, The workers lived in estate cottages and in what was a very close community. At Norman Court the Singers owned the whole of the villages of West Tytherley and West Dean, together with the outlying farms and cottages. The estate had its own sawmills and workshops and as far as possible equipment was made or mended on site. There was also an estate brickworks.

In areas where stone was not available locally, such as in the villages which surround Bentley Wood, cottages were traditionally either timber-framed, with wattle and daub infill, or made of chalk, or chalk and flint. Stone was reserved for churches and manor houses. Brick became fashionable for large houses in the 16th century but was not used for cheaper buildings at that time. The use of brick in cottages began with the construction of chimneys in timber-framed or chalk cottages, and from about 1800 onwards it was used increasingly for the whole building. On the Norman Court estate brick cottages date from the early 18th century onwards. Early examples have wide solid walls with rubble infill between two layers of brick.

Large estates frequently had their own brickworks and Norman Court was no exception. The West Dean brickworks, which probably started in the 1830s, was situated on the edge of Bentley Wood, off the road towards West Dean, where there was a seam of suitable clay. The site was also close to a good fuel supply, as large quantities of wood were needed to heat the kiln. A second kiln was added in the early 20th century.

In addition to bricks, the works produced roof tiles and drain tiles for local use. Throughout Britain fields on heavy ground had always been difficult to cultivate because of poor drainage and waterlogging but there had been no serious attempts to solve the problem before the 1820s. Small bore pipes, at a depth of about 4 feet, were then tried but were not very satisfactory. In 1843 the Royal Agricultural Society offered a silver medal for the best type of drain tile since much government money had been spent on assisting landowners to drain their land, with very poor results. Flat-bottomed horse-shoe drain tiles were the next attempt, which allowed the water to flow away well, but they were expensive to manufacture. Samples of these horse-shoe tiles were recovered from the Draining Field in Bentley Wood when it was reclaimed in 2002. Cylindrical, cheaper tiles soon followed and eventually were used universally. However, when they first came into use many farmers still wanted the horse-shoe tiles, believing that water could not possibly flow as well through a round one[4]!

West Dean brickworks closed down in 1945. By then bricks and tiles could be made more cheaply in large brickworks, and transported by road to all parts of the country. The clay workings can still be seen as a series of hollows on the edge of the wood.

The last days of Washington Singer.

Although Singer bought the estate in 1906, it was not until about 1910 that he came to regard his Norman Court mansion as his main residence. It was about this time that his first marriage came to an end with divorce. In 1915 he married a widow, Ellen Mary Longsdon, who already had several children from her first marriage. The younger children were legally adopted by Singer in 1927. Having suffered from prolonged illness, Washington Singer died in 1934. With the exception of Norman Court, which was inherited by his adopted son Grant once he became of age in 1936, the bulk of the estate, equivalent to about £46 million at present day values, went to his widow. Unfortunately, his adopted son Grant, the new owner of Norman Court and Bentley Wood, was killed in the battle of El Alamein in North Africa in 1942, and left no children.

10

World War II

For a few years during the 1940s normal life in Britain was suspended by World War II. Everyone had to carry an identity card and produce it on request, gas masks were issued in preparation for chemical warfare attacks, and total darkness, achieved by a variety of blackout measures, was the rule at night. The wail of air raid sirens, the noise of enemy aircraft overhead and the sound of anti-aircraft batteries were an all too frequent occurrence. Food rationing affected rich and poor alike, but it was perhaps a little easier to cope with in the country villages than in the towns. "Digging for Victory", or converting every inch of ground into a vegetable plot, and keeping a few chickens or rabbits to supplement the diet were easier in a country garden.

In general the countryside was a safer place to be in than the towns and cities, but the close proximity of military airfields and other potential targets for German bombing raids meant that the villages surrounding Bentley Wood sometimes saw rather more of enemy action than was comfortable. There were several military airfields within a 20 mile radius of the wood, including Middle Wallop, Old Sarum and Boscombe Down. Spitfire aircraft were assembled in Salisbury after devastatingly accurate air raids on the Supermarine factory in Southampton had halted production there, and the airfields at High Post and Chattis Hill were used for flight testing after assembly. On the hill to the north of Pitton village there was a decoy runway, which was one of a series of such decoys to draw attack away from the genuine airfields in the district.

Bentley Wood itself suffered very little damage from air attacks during the war, only one of the many pits in the wood is known to have been a bomb crater. It was formed when two land mines were dropped by a German bomber flying over the wood during the early years of the war. One of the mines landed in the northern section of Blackmoor Copse to the west of Bentley Wood, and the other landed on Cook's Common in the Hawksgrove part of the wood. The British Army Bomb Disposal Squad subjected both mines to controlled explosions. The crater created by the explosion on Cook's Common was enlarged, filled with water, and stocked with fish in the 1950-60s. Not surprisingly it became known as the "Bomb Pond".

At different times during the war, several aircraft crashed fairly close to the wood. On one occasion the residents of Pimlico, Winterslow, which was a row of 3 cottages on the edge of Bentley, were lucky not to be hit by a plane which crash-landed close by. At a different time another plane also came down in the same area on the eastern side of the wood.

Gordon Joyce, a resident of East Grimstead remembers, as a boy, cycling past a crashed German aircraft a few hundred yards from the southern edge of Bentley Wood, which was only a short distance from Dean Bomb Dump. In 1940 Roche Court, East Winterslow, was hit by a German bomber who jettisoned his bomb load before he flew on and crashed his aircraft near to the village of West Dean.

As the war progressed and the United States became involved, plans were made to launch a major invasion of the continent by the Allied Forces. This was a huge undertaking which involved the marshalling of all the troops from the different countries, together with their equipment, so that they were all present and prepared for action at the given moment. Southern Britain was chosen as the collecting area since it had the advantage of proximity to the area of conflict, and the short distance across the English Channel meant that invading troops could be given adequate air support. Decoy preparations were carried out in the south eastern corner of England, to suggest that an attack would be launched across the Dover Straits where the Channel is very narrow, but the real preparations were taking place further west.

During the build-up to D-Day, areas of woodland provided ideal camouflage for concentrations of soldiers with their camps, vehicles and equipment. Bentley Wood played its part and most of the wood to the north of the Howe Farm Track was requisitioned by the British War Department in preparation for US Army occupation. The British Army widened the Livery Track and laid a tarmac surface on it to provide a good access road. They also built accommodation huts which became known as Bentley Bungalows or Bentley Camp. A small number of trees was felled to create space for parking military vehicles and some areas were covered with gravel from Romsey Gravel Works to prevent sinking of heavier vehicles. Most of this gravel was eventually removed by the Forestry Commission for laying new tracks when replanting in the 1950-60s, but remnants can still be seen on the tracks and copses of Redman's Gore and Mapleway Dean today.

Norman Court mansion was used to house the 52nd AAA (Anti-Aircraft Artillery) Brigade Headquarters and American soldiers of several different battalions were located in Bentley at various times, while the NCOs lived in the huts of Bentley Camp. There was also a medical detachment, which nearly always accompanied AAA HQ Brigades, its "hospital" being a long Nissen hut erected close to the other huts in Bentley Camp. The brigade's location was officially described as "Norman Court" in US Army documentation. Marshalling areas such as Bentley Wood were often known as "sausage camps" because that is how they appeared on aerial photographs due to the shape of the Nissen huts arranged in rows. There were only two of the long type of Nissen huts in Bentley Camp but shorter versions were built in other parts of the wood. Telephone cables were laid to connect sentry boxes at the Livery Gate and Bentley Camp entrances with the Headquarters which was situated in the mansion itself. Field telephones were powered by portable electric batteries, and large generators were used to supply electricity for the camp kitchens and workshops.

Fig 39 *The American 'occupation' of Bentley Wood (R Pearce)*

Large woods like Bentley were chosen for their ability to conceal the army units from Luftwaffe reconnaissance aircraft. However, although woodland provided good cover for the large-scale build-up of troops, the protection was far from perfect and aerial photographs taken during the US occupation of Bentley Wood show quite clearly the lines of military vehicles present there.

When the first contingents of the US Army arrived in 1943 they came to a war-weary and gloomy country. The casualties and destruction of buildings by bombing raids were mounting and the people had endured a prolonged period of rationing of all basic commodities. Over half of the working population was either in uniform or civilian war employment, and the average working week was 50 hours. The arrival of the US soldiers provided a welcome diversion for the native population and they were generally well received in Britain. In country areas such as south Wiltshire it was often the first time that some of the villagers had seen black soldiers, who at that time were still segregated in separate units. The GIs were well provided for, they were better paid than their British counterparts and their camp shops were stocked very adequately. The Americans were usually generous to the local population, and being near to one of their bases often ensured a ready supply of food and other products which were in very short supply elsewhere.

Enterprising and curious local youngsters from Winterslow sometimes tried to penetrate into the northern part of Bentley Wood, but rarely got very far before being caught by the American patrols. The soldiers were usually tolerant and friendly with the boys, but persistent offenders found trying to start Jeeps, which did not need ignition keys to start their engines, were detained for the night. During the following day they would receive a severe reprimand from one of the officers in front of their parents. The presence of the US soldiers certainly enlivened the drab days for the local ladies in the villages around the wood, but, as in other parts of Britain, their appearance on the local dance floors was probably not always entirely welcomed by the local lads. The arrival of foreign troops into country areas usually put up prices in the local shops, and caused a shortage of alcohol but there were some compensations, such as Nylon stockings, good quality razor blades, American candy and the music of Glen Miller.

Further contingents of the US Army continued to arrive in the wood, building up to a peak shortly before D-Day in June 1944 and other nationalities also passed through the area, particularly Australians and Canadians. Daily life in

Bentley Camp was a heavy programme of training and the preparation of vehicles for the coming invasion. From the end of May 1944 all communication between troops and local residents was prohibited, and cyclists riding down the sides of Bentley Wood only ever saw the sentries on duty at the entrances.

In the immediate post-war years many parts of Bentley Wood were again used to store military vehicles and equipment returning from Europe. Eventually all was cleared away and redundant jeeps were sold to civilians to become useful farm vehicles. Some of the Nissen huts remained in use for many years as buildings on the estate. A vast amount of debris was buried in one or two of the chalk pits in the wood, US beer bottles, medicine containers, old shoes and parts of vehicles, which, when unearthed 50 years later, are an interesting reminder of the part played by Bentley Wood in the preparations for the invasion of occupied Europe.

11

The Forestry Commission

The Break-up of the Norman Court Estate

At the outbreak of World War II Britain was still heavily dependent on imported timber and although a considerable area of new forest had been established after the formation of the Forestry Commision, the new plantations were less than 20 years old. As in World War I, there were heavy losses of British merchant shipping which badly affected timber supplies, and in this war there were air raids as well. Not only were many buildings destroyed, but to make the situation worse some of the bombing raids destroyed stocks of timber and pitwood. As a result, large areas of both Forestry Commission and private woodland had to be felled. Extensive felling continued throughout the country during the early post-war years to meet the demand for timber, since there were still restrictions on importing it from abroad.

It was during this time that Norman Court and the whole estate was sold. The Singer family had already paid the government approximately £15 million (at present day values) in death duty tax in 1934. In 1942 Grant Singer, who had inherited the estate from his father, was killed at the age of 27 in the battle of El Alamein. He had no children and the only way that his widow could pay the second inheritance tax within 10 years was to sell the estate.

The mansion, all the estate houses and cottages, the farms, the village shops, two public houses and all the estate woodland were sold in separate lots. Two auctions were held in 1945 and 1946, which divided the sale over two years. Bentley Wood was split into lots for the auction and the sale catalogue gave a brief description of each, usually noting "with good standing timber". Some parts of the wood were still under requisition by the War Department when they were sold. The sales brochure included some general comments on the estate timber.

"Timber is one of the outstanding features of the Estate. The Woodland Lots should have very careful attention of Foresters and Timber Merchants as oak, ash, beech and other timber is particularly worthy of note, and the many Woodland Lots being offered with vacant possession, many of which occupy

delightful positions. The central portion of the Estate within the perimeter roads, has, except for the cutting of a small quantity of softwoods, been entirely untouched during the war years, and indeed for many generations previously, and provides some of the finest oak and beech to be found anywhere in the country. There is, however, a great deal of very valuable timber, oak, ash, Scotch and other varieties, standing on the lands outside the Copse on almost every lot."

Inevitably there was a considerable upheaval when two complete villages, West Tytherley and West Dean, were sold, as well as all the estate facilities. The estate houses and cottages were all sold separately, in many cases to sitting tenants. Unfortunately, some of the workers lost their livelihood when the estate was broken up and several were evicted from their tenancies under a court order, as they could not afford to buy their properties. A few of them found shelter in old Nissen huts for a year or so before moving into more suitable accommodation, all of which caused considerable hardship for those concerned.

A firm of timber merchants from Manchester, Reif and Son, bought both the mansion and Bentley Wood, together with some other parts of the estate. Along with the mansion house went "the Lordships, real or reputed, of the Manors of West Tytherley, Bentley Wood and West Dean", but it was only written in small print in the back of the sale brochure, and the timber merchant probably did not count Lordships as much of an asset anyway. Thus, the medieval manorial system was finally laid to rest. Shortly after buying the estate Reif and Son sold the parts which were of no interest to them, including the mansion, which later became a school. During the following four years the timber merchants felled many of the best quality timber trees in all parts of the wood. Bentley was then resold in 1950 and was acquired by the Forestry Commission.

At this point Bentley Wood appeared to be destined for a different kind of future than being part of a country estate. However, the sale of the wood to Reif was in many ways just history repeating itself. Timber was an essential commodity and it was in short supply, so large areas of woodland were felled to meet the immediate demand, and to make a profit. In previous centuries exactly the same had happened; medieval "waste" was the 20th century "clearfell". Successive kings had tried to control "waste" and only allowed very limited felling except under licence. In Tudor times laws were passed to ensure that 12 standard trees per acre were preserved after coppicing to allow for future supplies. None of the measures taken were particularly successful and there was always a chronic shortage in the country as a whole. In World War II and the years immediately following, timber was once again only felled under licence and the Forestry Commission also provided active encouragement to owners of private woodland to replant for the future. State ownership of some woodland to provide a reserve of timber had been necessary from the Norman Conquest right up to present times.

There were however, some essential differences. The scale on which the land was denuded in the clearfell, and the rapidity with which it was achieved, were far greater in the 20th century. The soil surface was also disturbed by heavy vehicles in a way that it would not have been in the past. In addition, there was a totally new school of thought as to how the wood should be restored and managed afterwards; plantations were seen as the way forward.

Fig 40 *Norman Court sale brochure, 1946. The estate forester with some of the timber. (HCRO ref 85M71PZ4)*

Fig 41 *Beech plantation in Bentley Wood. (A Baskerville)*

Fig 42 *Old oak tree and hazel stool in Bentley Wood today. (A Baskerville)*

Clear-fell and re-planting in the 1950s

When the future of forestry in Britain was considered after the war, it was proposed that 5 million acres should be the target for the country's forest area. This included both bare land which was to be newly afforested and also woodland to be re-planted and then managed in a more productive way than hitherto. Quite a proportion of the land was to remain in private hands, but the Forestry Commission would ensure that it was managed as productively as possible.

Under the Forestry Commission Bentley Wood became part of the national timber reserve for the future and the re-planting policy therefore reflected what was perceived to be the overall requirement for the country. Coniferous trees or softwoods (pines, spruces, larches and firs) predominated in the planting schemes in the 1950s because their timbers were required for most industrial and domestic use in preference to broadleaf trees, or hardwoods. In addition to sawn timber, used mainly for constructional purposes, softwoods were also used for pit-wood in coal mines, round poles and paper pulp. About half of the hardwood demand in the 1950s was for tropical timber such as mahogany which was imported from overseas. The two world wars had left Britain far more depleted in softwoods than hardwoods. Softwoods grow more quickly than hardwoods, and in the political and economic climate of the 1950s, this dictated the policy of the Forestry Commission to plant softwood species in preference to hardwoods. However, there were also a few important reasons for still planting a proportion of hardwoods. Good quality hardwood species, such as oak, attracted a higher price than softwood timber of an equivalent grade, a factor that is more important on private estates than in state-owned woodland. In the 1950s privately owned woodland was used for shooting and dense coniferous forests did not support as much game as broadleaf woodland. Other factors which governed the choice of plantation trees were local climate and soil type. The cooler upland areas of northern Britain favoured the growth of certain conifer species more than hardwoods. In lowland areas of southern Britain, especially recently cleared woodland like Bentley Wood, which was regarded as good quality growing land after the clear-fell, the Forestry Commission planted a much higher proportion of broadleaf species (about 50%) than in Scotland, Wales and northern England. In addition to all these factors, availability of transplant stock from local nurseries also played an important role in the choice of plantation tree species.

Most of the transplants planted in Bentley Wood by the Forestry Commission came from nurseries in Savernake Forest in north Wiltshire. At Savernake the young seedlings destined for Bentley spent the first two years in specially prepared seedbeds where they were carefully weeded. They were transplanted in the autumn-spring period, still in the Savernake nurseries, for a further year or two, and then transported to Bentley Wood, where they were re-planted into their final plantations. During very cold and frosty periods, which were unsuitable for planting, bundles of these transplants were buried temporarily in shallow soil, at an acute angle, to protect their roots from frost. A bushy root system was a good sign for future survival. Many of the transplants left the nurseries at 3-4 years old. Most of them ranged from 1-2 feet though the poplars planted in Barnridge Meadow were raised from cuttings and were about 5 feet tall when finally transplanted. Some of the seeds were home-grown, but others were imported from abroad. The larch came from Japan or Europe, Corsican pine from Corsica and Douglas fir from British Columbia. Before re-planting, the clear-felled ground was cleared of old root systems to improve soil conditions and assist drainage, and was checked for competing surface vegetation. A number of fire towers were erected in different parts of the wood, a few fragments of which remain today. The natural streams running through the wood were deepened and cleared to aid drainage, especially in Eastern Clearing and south of the Howe Farm track. Several new tracks were created to improve access to the plantations and some of the ancient tracks and boundaries were planted over, though many are still visible today.

The plantation crop of trees was very different from the oak-dominated coppice-with-standards, which had stood on Bentley Wood ground for many centuries. About 85% of the plantation compartments were planted with a mixture of broadleaf and conifers while the rest were planted with either pure conifer or broadleaf trees. Beech was the main broadleaf species planted on the chalky soils of the northern part of the wood (Fig. 41), and oak on the heavier acid clay soils in the southern areas. The trees were notch-planted, a procedure in which the transplant is inserted into a notch-shaped hole created by a planting spade. The mixtures consisted mainly of 3 rows of conifers to 3 rows of broadleaf but some areas were planted with a 3: 2 mixture. Occasional broadleaf groups were mixed with conifers in a diamond pattern, which looked attractive when viewed from the top of Dean Hill, but proved difficult to weed. The Forestry Commission's head forester decided on the planting ratios, in consultation with the area supervisor.

The complete re-planting of Bentley Wood covered a 30 year period from 1953 to 1983. It started in the central areas of the wood, Mapleway Dean and Redman's Gore, which had been partially cleared in the war years to cater for the US Army unit stationed there. Over 90% of the re-planting was completed by the early 1960s. The pure Corsican pine planting took place almost 20 years later (1979-83) in Barnridge Copse, Eastern Clearing, Park Copse, Cowley's Copse, Beechwood Copse and Dean Copse in the south of the wood. Later Corsican pine plantings may have been to replace crops of larch which had failed as a result of water-logging. There are very few larch to be seen in the wood today, although a few fine specimens can be found on the side of the Livery Track, near Bird-bath Junction. Less than 5% of the total area was left as open space when re-planting was complete, whereas pre-war aerial photographs suggest that a much greater area of the wood was open ground in the 1930s.

The initial clearing and re-planting of the wood took a long time. Reif and Son had already taken a considerable number of the best trees but those of poor commercial value, such as old coppice stools and willow trees, were still left standing. Contractors were engaged to clear whatever had been left, and they removed any trees which were saleable. The "rubbish" was then bulldozed together and burnt. A very small number of trees managed to escape the axe and the occasional old tree can still be seen around the wood today (Fig. 42).

The number of transplants planted by the Forestry Commission in Bentley Wood totalled about 4 million. The foresters were expected to plant 800-1000 per day. The men worked in rows, each man planting in a dead-straight line towards a different coloured marker, and they planted directly across most obstacles, including the pits. The new plantations were usually surrounded by wire netting to keep out rabbits, and rabbit trappers were employed when the wire failed to exclude them. Traces of this wire fencing can still be found, lying on the edges of some of the plantations. Rabbits were a major problem as they could devastate rows of newly planted trees and the cost and effort involved in protecting the plantations was considerable. The epidemic of myxomatosis, which decimated the rabbit population in the early 1950s, appeared to be the solution, but the population gradually increased again, although it was temporarily reduced from time to time by further outbreaks of the disease. Deer, which have since become so numerous in the wood, were far less common in the 1950s and they were nearly all roe deer.

Fig 43 *Tree felling in Bentley Wood today (D Lambert)*

Fig 44 *Modern forestry in Bentley Wood (A Baskerville)*

In some areas planting did not take place immediately after clearing the ground and a delay of up to 2 years allowed vigorous scrub, particularly birch and sallow, to grow up in the cleared space. When the time came for re-planting this new growth obstructed the planting operation. As time was short and money was shorter, "lanes" of clear ground were driven through the scrub for the trees to be planted. Unfortunately the "hedges", or remaining scrub between the lanes, grew faster than the trees and smothered the new plantation. Douglas fir planted in Richwellstead Copse did not grow very well in some parts due to the thin layer of chalky soil above solid chalk, and this copse was the first to be felled in the post-Forestry Commission days in 1984. However, at the base of the slope in this copse the soil was deeper and allowed better growth, so the firs growing here were left to grow and today make a magnificent stand of tall conifers.

The plantation work was carried out by a team of 6 or 7 foresters under the direction of the local head forester and between them they carried out the prodigious task of planting almost the entire wood and then looking after the trees. Additional help came from Savernake when extra teams of men were needed to assist with the weeding and spraying necessary to keep down the bramble and shrubby weeds between the rows.

The new forestry workers differed in many ways from the workforce which had trooped into the wood on winter mornings in Victorian times. Then coppice underwood had been sold in lots to independent woodsmen, who lived in the local villages and who spent the winter months cutting down the hazel, with the help of their families. They then sold the wood and coppice products to local dealers. The old woodsmen were not only highly skilled in coppice tasks but they also had a great knowledge and experience in estimating what a particular area of woodland would provide when harvested.

Creating and managing the new plantations required different skills and expertise, which included the use of a wide range of mechanical equipment and a knowledge of how to manage conifers as well as hardwoods. These new foresters often came from further afield, and not necessarily from the local village families. In contrast to the independent woodsmen of the past, each working on his own lot, they were employed as a structured team, with a Head Forester, and an Under Head Forester. There was also a Rabbit Trapper.

Since its inauguration the Forestry Commission had had a policy of providing local housing for their workforce and the housing programme continued after the war. A row of six houses was built on the edge of the wood in 1954 for the Bentley foresters, and the head forester and his men lived there with their families. In the 19th and early 20th centuries Norman Court had had its own forester, woodsmen and gamekeepers, who were housed in cottages provided by the estate. A typical such cottage is Pimlico, next to one of the entrances into Bentley Wood on the Tytherley Road, which was originally three cottages for woodsmen and gamekeepers.

The felling and re-planting were made possible by the use of equipment which had not been available in the past. Although mechanisation had begun with the Industrial Revolution, it was not until the 20th century that its real influence was felt in the woodland. Traditional methods continued as long as the traditional management of coppice and timber trees lasted, but felling and re-planting the entire wood called for a new approach. Motorised vehicles started to appear on the roads in the 1920s and tractors gradually replaced horses for farm work, though the horse still had a place in the woodland as it could drag wood out of difficult places, and did not plough up the ground. When tractors and bulldozers finally took over, the damage to the ground surface of the wood was considerable. New roads were urgently needed to allow access for such vehicles to and from the new plantations. In Bentley Wood some of the tracks had already been built up by the Army during the war, but others were made later under the Forestry Commission. The chainsaw replaced the old hand saws and axes in the late 1950s, and it revolutionised the task of felling timber. The sound of the chainsaw at work soon became one of the most familiar of sounds echoing across the woodland.

In the early days of re-planting the Forestry Commission encouraged charcoal burners to use up most of the hazel and other small trees before they started re-planting. The last major commercial production of charcoal in Bentley Wood took place in Howe Copse East in the period 1950-60 by the Valentine Timber Company from Southampton.

The predicted clear-fell date for most of the conifers planted by the Forestry Commission was estimated to be 2010-2020, although many of the trees will have been cut before then (in 2004 about 80% had already been cut). Usually 6-8 thinnings take place before the final crop reaches maturity and during this time about 80% of the original transplants are eliminated to create space for good growth of the remaining trees. The final target density for the oaks was estimated to be 125 trees per hectare (50 trees per acre) with an aim for clearfelling in the year 2070. The Forestry Commission in the 1950s predicted that the sale of conifers after 20 years' growth would pay for broadleaf thinnings, which were too small when first thinned to be of any commercial value. Also, the final crop was estimated at 1950 timber values to be worth twice as much as all the thinnings put together, because it consists of the largest and best stems, and timber values rise as the girth of logs increases. However, the economics of timber harvesting and sales has changed considerably since 1950 and these early estimates are no longer valid.

Walking through Bentley Wood today one often passes piles of sawn logs ready to be collected and transported to various sawmills and other destinations. The size of the logs depends on their intended use and the size of transport vehicles. Today, the present price of the usual timber species barely covers the cost of maintenance, cutting and transport. It is almost impossible to predict the long-term market and economics of a product such as timber, which may take 60-100 years to produce, and many factors can change in such a long period. In recent years, Britain's timber requirements have been increasingly met by importation because of the large scale of the forestry in other countries, which, coupled with lower labour costs and, in some cases, lower safety standards, makes production relatively cheaper. This is often compounded by unfavourable exchange rates. Before the early 1990s timber was leaving woodland at a profit for the woodland owner, but since then the value of home-grown timber has dropped, and now it provides little, if any, profit. In addition, the cost of weeding such a large area was much greater than had been realised at the outset. All these changes were unforeseen in the late 1940s when the Forestry Commission and the government were trying to plan for the future of British woodland.

Figs 45 *Male Purple Emperor (N Sampford)*

Fig 46 *Pearl- bordered Fritillary(N Sampford)*

12

Looking to the future

In 1983 Bentley Wood, together with many other plantation woodlands nationally, was put up for sale by the Forestry Commission as a result of a government directive. The proposed sale caused much anxiety as local people feared the access they had previously enjoyed would be curtailed or restricted. Furthermore, the conservation movement of the time, then growing in authority, was concerned that any sale of the Wood would endanger the unique assemblage of flora and fauna that inhabited the site.

Fortunately the late Lady Ann Colman, of Middleton Manor, Winterslow, intervened at a critical juncture and through great foresight and generosity established a charitable trust and enabled it to buy Bentley Wood, thus ensuring that it would be protected from the whims and foibles of a private landowner. Sadly, Lady Colman died before her intentions for the wood could be established but, through the trust and the responsibility placed on the Trustees by Lady Colman, the future of Bentley Wood as a mature and beautiful woodland is assured. It is a place to which people will always have access and where their wishes and opinions, especially those of local people, will be heard and respected.

During the early years, Ralph Whitlock, well known broadcaster and writer, was fundamental to the success of the Trust. Ralph, from a local family, was appointed founder Trustee and 'guardian' of the Wood by Lady Colman. His unstinting devotion to Bentley Wood and enthusiasm during the formative years were well demonstrated by his ability to persuade a great number of both amateur and professional naturalists, together with many volunteers locally, to contribute their expertise and valuable time to Bentley Wood. But perhaps Ralph's greatest achievement was his founding of the Friends of Bentley Wood. The 'Friends' are a group of local people who share Ralph's love of the Wood, and whose tireless contributions are still appreciated greatly today.

At the time of sale it was known that the importance of Bentley Wood's natural history was shortly to become recognised through its designation as a Site of Special Scientific Interest (SSSI). The interests and needs of the plants and other wildlife would require special attention, with priority given to the butterflies and moths which were specifically mentioned in the designation. Into the foreseeable future, therefore, it will be the Trustees' duty to strike the best balance between the interests of forestry, wildlife and people.

Forestry operations over the last twenty years have followed the textbook procedure of the regular thinning of plantations and the removal of the conifer nursery crop. In the early years softwood thinnings provided a useful source of income and much of this nursery crop was removed. Latterly, however, competition in the form of cheap imports from eastern Europe has depressed timber sales, and markets - particularly for softwoods - are becoming increasingly difficult to find. Fortunately, in the light of ever-increasing energy costs, a reliable market remains in the form of firewood for the hardwood thinnings and, while this market exists, thinning of oak in the south and beech in the north of the Wood will continue until final crop spacing is achieved. Recent guidelines on the management of plantations on ancient woodland sites support the policy of thinning hardwood stands 'little and often' if wind blow is to be avoided and a diverse ground flora maintained. However, as the Wood was replanted over a short time-scale an even age structure has resulted and therefore in certain areas heavy thinnings and premature clearfells will be undertaken to encourage a more diverse age structure through natural regeneration and the occasional planting of native species. Deer browsing is, and will continue to be, a problem here as it is across much of southern England. Indeed deer browsing is considered to be one of the greatest threats facing the future of woodlands in Britain. This, of course, is nothing new; in 1482 Edward IV passed a statute authorising the enclosure of woods by various means to keep out browsing and grazing animals.

Managing for wildlife is a less than exact science and often over the years Bentley Wood has found itself at the forefront of habitat and species conservation techniques. Bentley Wood has two advantages here. First and foremost the Wood remains a commercially viable operation. The flora and fauna that together make Bentley Wood such a special place are the direct result of centuries of active woodland management through coppicing of the underwood and management of the high forest. Many species now considered rare or declining, both locally and nationally, have survived in Bentley Wood because coppicing has been continued, rides maintained and clearings created. Secondly, Bentley Wood is vast and this affords the opportunity to manage different areas in different manners. For example the low intensity grazing

Fig 47 *Ralph Whitlock, founder trustee and 'guardian' of the wood.(Salisbury Newspaper Group)*

recently initiated in Barnridge is helping to restore an area of ancient meadow, and if successful could well be implemented in other parts of the Wood. Similarly, heavy thins initiated in the beech in the north of the Wood will be repeated elsewhere if they are proven to benefit ground flora and natural regeneration. Much of the remaining ancient woodland flora, that is plants that are only found in woodlands with a long history of continuous tree cover, today only survive in patches, commonly along the woodland edge and other areas where the woodland floor has not been damaged by heavy machinery. Sympathetic management and a lot of time will be needed if the ancient woodland flora is to recolonise the plantations deeper within the wood.

Historically the creation of large clearings through clearfelling the high forest and coppicing of the underwood provided the early successional habitats much favoured by the woodland butterflies and moths. Although coppicing continues, albeit at a much lower intensity than in the past, large areas of high forest are not yet old enough to be harvested on a large scale and therefore in recent years the ride systems in Bentley Wood have provided a refuge of open space for these species, many of which have been lost from surrounding woodland. Some, but not all rides, will continue to be managed on a rotation - with wildlife in mind - for the foreseeable future.

We live in an age that has witnessed the decline of many rural crafts, skills and traditions. The sight of a dozen or so woodsmen trudging down Lower Road in Winterslow early each morning is still within the living memory of some local people. Nowadays those people visiting the wood in the early hours are more likely to be exercising dogs before driving to work in nearby towns and cities. Such has been the change in the countryside across rural England since the Second World War. However, where possible the Trustees consider it their responsibility to play a role in ensuring that certain traditional woodland crafts such as charcoal burning, spar and hurdle making, that were so fundamental to both the wildlife and local community in the past, are continued and encouraged where markets allow. Similarly, the vast network of woodland banks, pits, lynchets, sunken tracks, settlements and other remaining archaeological features, evidence of past centuries of husbandry, are also to be preserved wherever possible.

It is, however, for butterflies and moths that Bentley Wood is best known outside the local community and the wood continues to witness large numbers of visiting butterfly enthusiasts from all over the country in search of species that have been lost from their region. Bentley Wood is perhaps best known as a place to view the majestic Purple Emperor. (Fig. 45).

SSSIs are commonly designated by habitat type such as ancient woodland or chalk downland, but Bentley Wood was specifically notified because of the unusually large number of rare butterfly and moth species breeding within its boundaries. This citation has been justified over the last twenty years or so as many of the species listed in the notification have declined or disappeared from woodlands across much of the rest of the country. SSSI status currently demands that the Wood be returned to what is termed 'favourable condition', that being something akin to what Bentley looked like in the years before the clearfell of the 1940s and 1950s, and we are fortunate that advice from many conservation bodies together with the provision of grants from statutory authorities, particularly English Nature, Forestry Commission and DEFRA, have made it possible to manage the Wood to this end in a climate where forestry sales are much reduced. We live in an age when the sustainability of

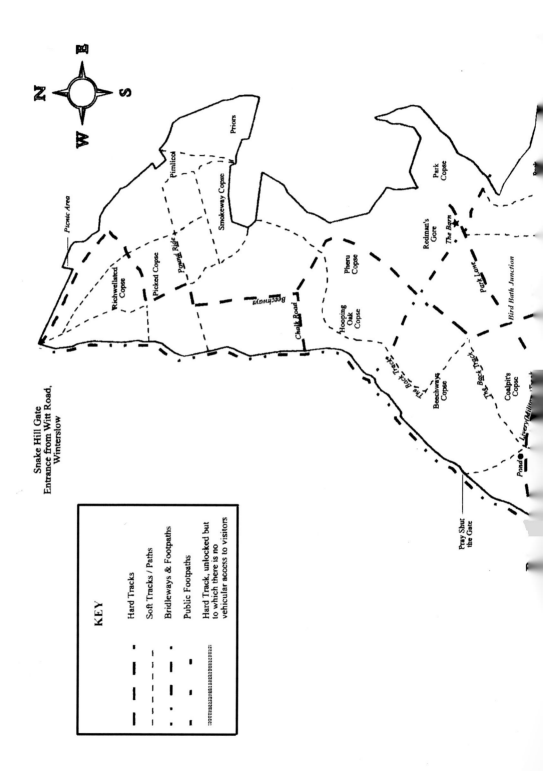

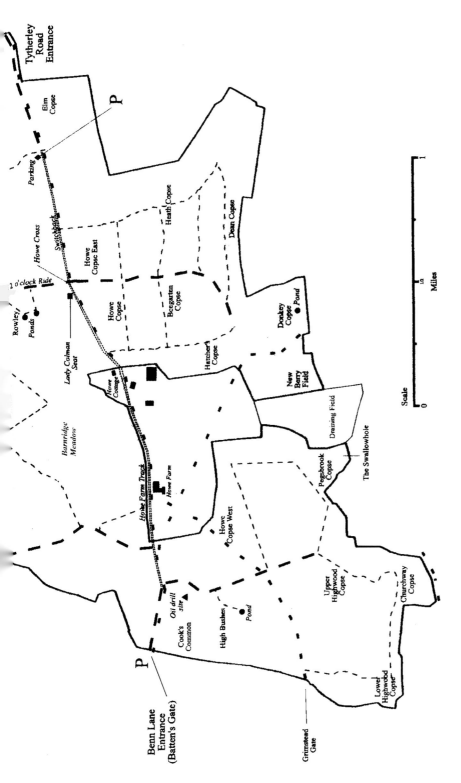

Fig 48 *Bentley Wood today, showing modern names, tracks and other features.*

many traditional land management practices are in doubt. Conservation and amenity now top the agenda. The Trustees have, and will always have, difficult decisions to make between managing for known present day gains for grants and against future possible gains from timber sales. However, following these guidelines it is hoped that Lady Colman's intentions will be achieved and Bentley Wood will remain a wonderful place for both wildlife and people.

If British Woodlands are to regain some of their former diversity, then it is essential that their owners incorporate appropriate aims into their management policies. Sadly, at a time when revenue from timber is low, few will have the resources to do this, unless government grants are maintained at high levels for the forseeable future. Our dreams of fifteen years ago, of being able to maintain woodlands in a sustainable fashion and, at the same time, improve their conservation value, seem to have faded. There may well be difficult decisions to be made - short-term gains from harvesting versus keeping trees past their maturity (in terms of timber production) for conservation purposes. Our forefathers showed much insight when they planted for future generations; something not generally shared by today's custodians of the countryside and of our natural resources. Let us hope that Lady Colman's wishes will be fulfilled and Bentley Wood will develop something of its former glory. If, in achieving this, other woodland owners and managers can be helped to improve their land, then the rewards will be even greater.

Appendix I

Woodland Terms

Afforest. To designate an area as forest (see below).

Assart. An area of ground in a forest which has been cleared by pulling up the tree roots to make agricultural land.

Barking. The removal of bark from felled oak trees, which was then used for tanning leather.

Bavin. A bundle of untrimmed brushwood used as fuel in kilns and kitchen fires.

Common rights. Common land belonged to the landowner, or lord of the manor. The occupiers of certain properties in the area had specified rights on the common land, such as grazing for their animals or collecting firewood.

Coppice. Trees which were cut almost to ground level forming a stool, from which re-growth occurred. The wood could be harvested every few years. Coppice-with-standards was an area of coppice with some timber trees.

Faggot. A bundle of brushwood or sticks used as fuel for houses or kilns.

Forest. An area subject to Forest Law. It was not necessarily woodland. The land could be in private hands but the owners were restricted as to what they could do with it. Many forests were Crown land.

Forester. An officer who administered Forest Law in the royal forests under the warden. The chief foresters were the foresters-in–fee, who were in charge of sub-divisions of the forest.

Forest eyre. A court held by itinerant judges to settle forest matters, and to deal with offences against Forest Law.

Lawing (or expedition). The removal of three toes on one forefoot of a dog. It had to be carried out on all mastiffs owned by people dwelling within a forest to prevent the dog from catching deer.

Lug(g). A linear measurement of land, most commonly $16\frac{1}{2}$ feet, the same as a rod, pole or perch. It could also be 15 or 18 feet.

Pannage. The right to turn pigs out into woodland, or wood-pasture, in the autumn to feed on the acorns and beech mast.

Perambulation. An official inspection of the boundaries of a forest to ensure that the limits had not been altered.

Pollard. A tree which is cut at 8-12ft. above ground and allowed to grow again to produce successive crops of wood. At this height browsing animals cannot reach the new growth.

Regarders. The twelve officers who were appointed for each forest to supervise local forest officers. They held a "regard", or inspection, every third year to report on the state of the forest and to enquire into offences against Forest Law.

Shrouding. Removal of the side branches of pollards.

Teller. A young tree suitable for future timber.

Underwood. Wood which was repeatedly cropped as coppice or pollards to produce poles.

Vert. Trees and undergrowth which provided food for the deer.

Warden. The head officer in charge of the administration of a royal forest. It was originally a hereditary office.

Waste. The cutting down of woodland within a forest without a licence to do so. "Waste" was also used to mean rough grazing land.

Wood-pasture. Grazing land with some trees. The trees were often pollarded, rather than coppiced, to prevent damage to the young growth by grazing animals.

Woodward. An officer appointed by the owner of a wood within a royal forest to look after the "vert and venison".

Useful explanations of other woodland words can be found in: "A Historical Dictionary Of Forest And Woodland Terms" by NDG James (1991) Blackwell.

Appendix II

Valuation of Bentley Wood 1813

Valuation for Amesbury estate.

WCRO ref 995/4

Coalpits coppice. With the lane adjoining.

355 oak trees
643 oak tellers
470 ditto
165 ditto
147 ditto
1 maple
4 ash trees
2 beech trees
48 acres of underwood of 2 years growth.
Total value of timber, tellers and underwood £901 2s 1p.

Rowley coppice and the lane adjoining.

95 oak trees
600 oak tellers
572 ditto
41 ditto
230 ditto
74 acres of underwood of 5 years growth.
Total value £641 1s 6p.

Hermitage coppice

426 oak trees
552 oak tellers
260 ditto

105 ditto
231 ditto
6 ash trees
49 acres of underwood of 6 years growth.
Total value £112 6s 9p.

Red Ridge and lane adjoining

1198 oak trees
1044 oak tellers
78 ditto
128 ditto
722 ditto
36 beech trees
5 ash trees
87 acres of underwood of 13 years growth.
Total value   £3676 19s 6p.

Mapleway Dean

277 oak trees
641 oak tellers
381 ditto
57 ditto
333 ditto
52 acres of underwood.
Total value £842 15s 0p.

Beechway coppice and the lane adjoining.

536 oak trees
988 oak tellers
489 ditto
90 ditto
534 ditto
2 ash trees

20 beech trees
96 acres of underwood of 3 years growth.
Total value £1426 16s.

Hooping Oak coppice with part of Riding Lane.

277 oak trees
885 oak tellers
279 ditto
87 ditto
25 ditto
7 ash trees
4 beech trees
59 acres of underwood of 9 years growth.
Total £1190 19s.

Redman Gore and part of Park Lanc.

453 oak trees
1000 oak tellers
314   ditto
44   ditto
314   ditto
2 beech trees
50 acres of underwood of 1 years growth.
Total value £946 16s 1p.

Priors coppice with part of Park Lane.

250 oak trees
650 oak tellers
250   ditto
79   ditto
240   ditto
181 beech trees
61 acres of underwood of 11 years growth.
Total value £1302 3s 9p.

Smoakway coppice

388 oak trees
520 oak tellers
285 ditto
87 ditto
320 ditto
9   ash trees
4   beech trees
6   ash
54 acres of underwood of 7 years growth.
Total value £971 12s 3p.

Three Sisters coppice with part of Riding Lane.

352 oak trees
848 oak tellers
268 ditto
90 ditto
190 ditto
2   beech trees
1   ash
53 acres of underwood of 8 years growth.
Total value £1147 19s.

Picked coppice with part of Riding Lane.

392 oak trees
500 oak tellers
200 ditto
80 ditto
175 ditto
42 beech trees
2 ash
62 acres of underwood of 10 years growth.
Total value £1357 13s 1p.

Appendix III

Extracts from the book of John Parsons

John Parsons   His Book
September the 25th 1767
My name is set hear to betray the thief that steal my book

Hawksgrove Dec 7th 1782

95 Lugs of standing wood	4	10	0
Hawksgrove Feb 1st 1783			
Samuel Light for 80 lugs of			
standing wood	4	0	0
Hawksgrove Feb 3rd 1783			
Joseph Hatcher jun for 21 lugs			
of standing wood	0	19	0
1784 Nov 12			
Coalpits coppice First side 192 lugs			
In the 20 Mr Bloxam	8	18	0
The Left side Ditto 168 lugs	8	15	0
Mr Brown			
Nov 13 1784			
Barnridge Mr Bloxam 529 lugs		13	6
Ditto Mr Brown ? lugs			

(1783)

Hawksgrove May 12 John Davies for wood	0	12	0
May 13 Thomas Clark 150 round faggets	0	16	6
May 26 Ann Williams 225 peny faggets	0	16	0
May 28 Edward London 150 peny faggets	0	18	0
May 28 Joseph Hatcher for wood	0	5	6
May 29 Mr Collis 250 peny faggets	1	7	6
June 2 Mr Collis 250 peny faggets	1	7	6
June 3 Mr Collis 250 peny faggets	1	7	6
June 2 John Stickland 175 Round faggets	0	19	3
June 3 Wm Lodge 100 bavens	0	4	0
June 4 Joseph Calaway 175 round faggets	0	19	3

June 4 Samull London 150 Round faggets	0	18	0
June 4 Job Sanders 150 Round faggets	0	18	0
May 31 John Callaway 150 Round faggets	0	18	0
June 5 Mr Collis 250 peny faggets	1	7	6
June 5 Wm ? 175 Round faggets	0	19	3
June 6 John Hall 175 Round faggets	0	19	3
June 6 John Hayes 50 bavens	0	2	0
June 7 Richard Harnam 175 Round faggets	0	19	3
June 9 John Stickland 175 Round faggets	0	19	0
June 9 Mr Rendle 250 peny faggets	1	7	6
June 9 Peter Rombold 300 peny faggets	1	1	9

Coalpits Copse March 4 1785

	£	s	d
Mr Sutten 100 bundles of Bushes	0	10	0
For 70 Lugs of row wood & Cutting	4	4	0
March 12 for 110 bundles of Bushes	0	11	0
March 16 50 Round faggets	0	5	6
Loading Row	0	1	0
May 11 1 Load of row wood	0	12	0
May 12 12000 of Spars	0	16	0
Ditto for Row wood	0	3	0
May 16 for 200 peny faggets g 500 spars	1	8	8
25 250 peny faggets	1	0	0
June 14 200 peny faggets	0	16	0
200 peny faggets	0	16	0
2500 Spars	0	3	4
	11	16	10

(1783)

Hawksgrove May12 John Davies for wood	0	12	0
May 13 Thomas Clark 150 Round faggets	0	16	6
May 26 Ann Williams 225 peny faggets	0	16	0
May 28 Edward London 150 peny faggets	0	18	0
May 28 Joseph Hatcher for wood	0	5	6
May 29 Mr. Collis 250 peny faggets	1	7	6
June 2 Mr. Collis 250 peny faggets	1	7	6
June 3 Mr. Collis 250 peny faggets	1	7	6
June 2 John Stickland 175 Round faggets	0	19	3

June 3 Wm Lodge 100 bavens	0	4	0
June 4 Joseph Calaway 175 Round faggets	0	19	3
June 4 Job Sanders 150 Round faggets	0	18	0
May 31 John Callaway 150 Round faggets	0	18	0
June 5 Mr. Collis 250 peny faggets	1	7	6
June 5 Wm ? 175 Round faggets	0	19	3
June 6 John Hall 175 Round faggets	0	19	3
June 6 John Hayes 50 bavens	0	2	0
June 7 Richard Harnam 175 Round faggets	0	19	3
June 9 John Stickland 175 Round faggets	0	19	0
June 9 Mr. Rendle 250 peny faggets	1	7	6
June 9 Peter Rombold 300 peny faggets	1	1	0

Appendix IV

Extract from Seymour papers at
Longleat House, volume 12.

Rent Roll of Edward Seymour, Viscount Beauchamp, afterwards Duke of Somerset and Lord Protector, 1540, folios 255-256:

Woods called Bentley Woods-

A Copse callyd Collpytts copse is of xvi yeres growth and conteyneth xxx acres
A Copse callyd Redm'more is of xvii yeres growth and conteyneth xx acres
A Copse callyd Pykkyd Copse is of xv yeres growth and conteyneth xxx acres
A Copse callyd Haysley is of xiiii yeres growth and conteyneth xx acres
A Copse callyd Fayre yewe is of xiiii yeres growth and conteyneth xxvi acres
A Copse callyd Reddrydge is of xi yeres growth and conteyneth lv acres
A Copse callyd Pryers Copse is of xi yeres growth and conteyneth xx acres
A Copse callyd Whoping Oke is of ix yeres growth and conteyneth xxx acres
A Copse callyd Ou'beche ways is of viii yeres growth and conteyneth xx acres
A Copse callyd Nether beche ways is of v yeres growth and conteyneth xx acres
A Copse callyd iii Systers and Smokkways is of iiii yeres growth and conteyneth L acres
A Copse callyd Barne Rydge is of iii yeres growth and conteyneth xxx acres
A Copse callyd Rammyshyll Copse is of two yeres growth and conteyneth xx acres
A Copse callyd Maple Dene is of one yeres growth and conteyneth xxi acres
A Copse callyd Nods is of div's yeres growing and conteyneth xii acres
A Copse callyd Armytage Copse is of vii yeres growth and conteyneth xx acres

Item: The said copse callyd Nods conteynyng by estimacion xii acres hathe be allowed long tyme to the kings teneants for mounting and hedging always as need requyryd

The comens within this said manor hereafter foloweth-
A comen callyd Rammyshyll Playn conteyneth xl acres

A comen callyd Rowley grene and Black mare hyll conteyneth xx acres
A comen callyd Dene heth conteyneth c(?) acres
A comen callyd mery grove corn' xii acres
A comen callyd Brode Lees and Pre…(?) Gore conteyneth xvi acreas

Item: Of all that forsaid comens the kings majesty always takyth the…of the oke and underwood in the time past and the pasture and ground that notwithstanding is usyd in comen to all the tenants there

NB. Nodes, Ramshill and Haysley (Ashley) coppices, which are in East Winterslow, also belonged to Amesbury Manor.

Abbreviations

OS   Ordnance Survey
HCRO   Hampshire County Record Office
WCRO   Wiltshire County Record Office
PRO   Public Record Office
VHH   Victoria History of Hampshire
VHW   Victoria History of Wiltshire

References

Chapter One

1. Rackham,O. (1986) Woodland. *The history of the countryside. 62-118. Dent, London.*
2. Cunliffe,B. (1993) *Wessex to AD 1000.* 5-35. Pearson Education, Harlow.
3. Dark,P. (2000) *The environment of Britain in the 1st millennium AD.* 34-80. Duckworth, London.

Chapter Two

1. Salway,P. (1981) Roman Britain (The Oxford History of England) p 624. Oxford Univ. Press.
2. Dark,P. (2000) *The environment of Britain in the 1st millennium* AD. 81-129. Duckworth, London.
3. VHW (1973) **1** p448.
4. Master,G.S. (1885) Collections for a history of West Dean. *Wilts. Archeol. and Nat. Hist. Mag.* **14** 239-316.
5. Sumner,H. (1924) *Excavations at East Grimstead, Wiltshire.*
6. Rackham,O. (1986) *The history of the countryside.* p74. Dent, London.
7. Grundy,G.B. (1938) The ancient woodland of Wiltshire. *Wilts. Archeol. and Nat. Hist. Mag.* **48** 530-598.
8. Dark,P. (2000) *The environment of Britain in the 1st millennium* AD. 19-33. Duckworth, London.
9. Master,G.S. (1872) Roman remains found at Holbury near Dean. *Wilts. Archeol. and Nat. Hist. Mag.* **13** 33-42.

Chapter Three

1. Grundy,G.B. (1938) The ancient woodland of *Wiltshire. Wilts. Archeol. and Nat. Hist. Mag.* **48** 530-598.
2. *The calendar of patent rolls.* 1485-94.
3. VHW (1956) **3** The religious houses of Wiltshire.
4. Colt Hoare,R. (1825) **2** Amesbury. *The modern history of Wiltshire.*
5. VHH (1973) **2** Forestry and the New Forest.
6. Watts,M. (1999) *Working oxen.* Shire publications.
7. Inquisitiones post mortem relating to Wiltshire from the reign of Edward III. Part 2. Idonea de Leybourne 1334. *Wilts. Archeol. and Nat. Hist. soc.* (1910)

8. Trow Smith,R. (1957) Saxon settlement and the Domesday survey. *A history of British livestock to 1700.* Routledge, London.

9. *The farmer's library.(circa 1850)* **2** Animal economy. p436.

10. Pugh,R.B. (1947) *The calendar of Antrobus deeds before 1625.* No. 100.

11. *Antrobus deeds* (as above) No. 128.

12. *Antrobus deeds* (as above) No. 138.

13. *Estate map of Amesbury manor.* WCRO ref. 994/1-2

14. Colt Hoare,R. (1837) **5** Alderbury. *The modern history of Wiltshire.*

15. Wordsworth,C. (1902) The charter of Countess Ela, 1227. In *The 15th century cartulary of St. Nicholas' Hospital.*

16. Dean Wood. WCRO ref. 727/13/10.

17. As 15. p279.

18. WCRO ref. 1672/6/1

19. WCRO ref. 1672/5/7

20. VHH (1911) **4** West Tytherley.

21. Master,G.S. (1885) Collections for a history of West Dean. *Wilts. Archeol. and Nat. Hist. Mag.* **22** 239-316.

22. Watts,K. (1998) *Exploring historic Wiltshire.* **2** p163. Ex Libris Press, Bradford on Avon.

23. *The endowed charities of Wiltshire.* (1907) 88-89.

24. WCRO ref. 1300/104

Chapter Four

1. Rackham,O. (1986) *The history of the countryside.* p133. Dent, London.

2. Muir,R. (2000) *The new reading the landscape.* p16. Univ. Press, Exeter.

3. Parsons,M. (1998) *All the king's men.* p40. Parsons, New Milton, Hants.

4. VHW (1959) **4** Forests.

5. Colt Hoare,R. (1837) **5** Clarendon Forest. *The history of modern Wiltshire.*

6. Garnet,C. (1997) Conquered England. In *The Oxford illustrated history of medieval England.* Ed. Saul,N. Oxford Univ. Press.

7. Ashley,M. (1972) *The life and times of King John.* 158-203. Weidenfeld and Nicolson and Book Club Associates.

8. Powicke, M. (1962) *The 13th century 1216-1307.* 644-718. Oxford Univ. Press.

9. Rackham,O. (1986) *The history of the countryside.* p87. Dent, London.

10. Parsons,M. (1997) *The brittle thread.* p23. Parsons, New Milton, Hants.

11. VHH (1973) **2** Forestry and the New Forest.

Chapter five

1. Inqisitiones post mortem relating to Wiltshire from the reign of Edward III. Part 2. Idonea de Leybourne 1334. *Wilts. Archeol. and Nat. Hist. Soc.* (1910).

2. Grundy,G.B. (1938) The ancient woodland of Wiltshire. *Wilts. Archeol. and Nat. Hist. Mag.* **48** 530-598.

3. Parsons,M. (2001) *Atrocious deeds.* p80. Parsons, New Milton, Hants.

4. Rackham,O. (1989) *The last forest.* p91. Dent, London.

5. Rackham,O. (1986) *The history of the countryside.* 62-118. Dent, London.

6. PRO refs. Eyre 1262-3 (E32/199) and Eyre 1330 (E32/207).

7. PRO ref. E32/200.

8. Pollard,A.J. (2000) *Late medieval England 1399-1509.* 169-194. Longman.

9. Rackham,O. (1986) *The history of the countryside.* 153-155. Dent, London.

10. Whitlock,R. (1977) *A short history of farming.* 104-167. Routledge, London.

11. WCRO ref 1672/5/7

12. WCRO ref. 1300/104.

Chapter Six

1. Chandler,J. (1988) *The printed maps of Wiltshire.* Wilts. Record Soc.

2. Amesbury estate map 1726. WCRO ref 994/1-2.

3. Map of Dean Wood. WCRO ref. 727/13/ 10.

4. A survey of Norman Court and Broughton estates. HCRO ref. 85M71PZ2.

5. Estate map of West Dean manor. WCRO ref. 2932/6.

6. Map of the Earl of Radnor's estate of Farley Farm. WCRO ref. 1946/H32.

7. Kain,R.J.P. and Prince,H.C. (2000) *Tithe surveys for historians.* 31-71. Phillimore, Chichester.

8. Ellis,W. (1772) *Ellis's Husbandry* **1.** 49-54.

9. Hampshire Countryside Heritage. (1983) **2** Ancient woodland. Hants. Co.Council.

10. Hill,R. and Stamper,P. (1993) *The working countryside.* 133-145. Swan Hill Press.

11. Report of the commissioners of the woods and forests, 1783-1789. (1793) Appendix 2, Hants.

12. VHH (1973) **2** Forestry and the New Forest.

13. Cobbett,W. (1882) *Rural rides.*

14. Stamp,L.D. (1955) *Man and the land.* 187-204. New Naturalist **31** Collins, London.

15. James,N.D.G. (1990) *A history of English forestry.* Blackwell, Oxford.

16. Valuation and survey of Amesbury estate (1831) WCRO ref. 995/3.

17. Whitlock,R. (1990) *The Victorian village.* 136-152. Robert Hale, London.

18. Parsons,M. (2001) *Life in a Victorian parish.* Parsons,New Milton, Hants.

19. Forest eyre with inquisition, 1256-57. PRO ref. E32/198.

20. Niall,I. (1950) *The poacher's handbook. Heinemann, London.*

21. WCRO ref. 1672/5/7.

22. WCRO ref. 283/183.

23. WCRO ref. 283/171.

24. WCRO ref. 776/1122.

25. HCRO ref. 101M96/3.

26. HCRO ref. 101M/96/3/1-14.

Chapter Seven

1. Gower,J.E.B. Mawer,A. and Stenton,F.M. (1970) *The place-names of Wiltshire.* The English Place-Name Soc. **16** Cambridge Univ. Press.

2. Master,G.S. (1885) Collections for a history of West Dean. *Wilts, Archeol. and Nat. Hist. Mag.* **22** 239-316.

3. Map of Amesbury estate, 1726. WCRO ref. 994/1-2.

4. Cameron,K. (1988) *English place-names.* Batsford, London.
5. Map of Dean Wood (circa *1800*) WCRO ref. 727/13/10.
6. Parsons,M. (1994) *The parish tithe award.* p2. Parsons, New Milton, Hants.
7. Gelling,M. (1994) *Place-names in the landscape.* Phoenix, London.
8. VHW (1959) **4** p428.
9. Letter to the Earl of Hertford, 1614. WCRO ref. 1672/5/7.
10. West Dean estate map, 1820. WCRO ref. 2932/6.
11. Muir,M. (2000) *The new reading the landscape.* p64. Univ. Press, Exeter.
12. Colt Hoare,R. (1837) **5** Clarendon Forest. *The history of modern Wiltshire.* p132.
13. Parsons,M. (1995) *The royal forest of Pancet.* p45. Parsons, New Milton, Hants.
14. Rent roll of Edward Seymour, Viscount Beauchamp, afterwards Duke of Somerset, folios 255-256 (1540) from the Seymour papers at Longleat House, **12**.

Chapter eight

1. Tubbs,C.R. (2001) *The New Forest.* p281. New Naruralist **73** Collins, London.
2. Rackham,O. (1986) *The history of the countryside.* 345-373. Dent, London.
3. Gosnell,R. (2003) The geology of Bentley Wood. *Bentley Wood nature notes.* p13.
4. Sumner,H.(1924) *Excavations at East Grimstead, Wiltshire.*
5. Parsons,M. (1994) *The parish tithe award.* p49 Parsons, New Milton, Hants.
6. Ellis,W. (1772) *Ellis's husbandry.* 50-51.
7. Dyer,C. (2000) Woodlands and wood pasture in western England. In *Rural England.* 97-121. Ed. Thirsk,J. Oxford Univ. Press.

Chapters Nine and Eleven

1. Parsons,M (1997) *The brittle thread.* 52-55. Parsons, New Milton, Hants.
2. Parsons,M. (1999) *Chips and chumps.* 39-61. Parsons, New Milton, Hants.
3. Whitlock,R. (1998) *The lost village.* 61-63. Robert Hale, London.
4. Portious,C. (c1920) The drainers. In *Pioneers of fertility. ICI.*
5. Hony,G.B. (1926) Sheep farming in Wiltshire, with a short history of the Hampshire Down breed. *Wilts. Archeol. and Nat. Hist. Mag.* **43** 449-464.

Bibliography
James,N.D.G. (1990) *A history of English forestry.* Blackwell, Oxford.
Edlin,H.L. (1956) *Trees, woods and man. New Naturalist* **32** Collins, London.

Chapter Ten

Bibliography
1. Hall,T. (2001) *D-Day; the strategy, the men, the equipment. Salamander Books.*
2. Healy,T. (1993) *Life on the home front.* Readers Digest Assoc.
3. Berryman,D. (2002) *Wiltshire airfields in the second World War.* Countryside Books, Newbury.